A a *a*

a

Jack has **a** dog.
He has one dog.
Jill has **a** cat.
She has one cat.

A cat and **a** dog.

above

Twinkle, twinkle, little star.
How I wonder what you are.
Up **above** the world so high,
Like a diamond in the sky.

The star is in the sky. It is high up.
It is **above** Jack and Jill.

accident

Jack and Jill went up the hill
    To fetch a pail of water.
Jack fell down and broke his crown,
    And Jill came tumbling after.

Jack and Jill fell down.
They did not mean to fall.
They had an **accident**.

act

Jack and Jill are at a Punch and Judy show. They want to see Punch and Judy **act**. Punch and Judy will play a part. They will be acting. They are actors.

Jack will pay for Jill.
He will do her a good turn.
It will be a kind **act**.

add

If you put one and one together, you have two.
You **add** one and one together.

Put salt in the soup.
Add salt to the soup.

You have added salt.

address

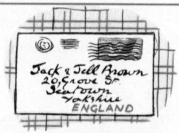

This is their **address**.

Jack has the same **address** as Jill. They both live in the same house.

Where do you live?
What is your **address**?

aeroplane

Jack has a toy **aeroplane**.
A real aeroplane flies through the air.
It is a flying machine.

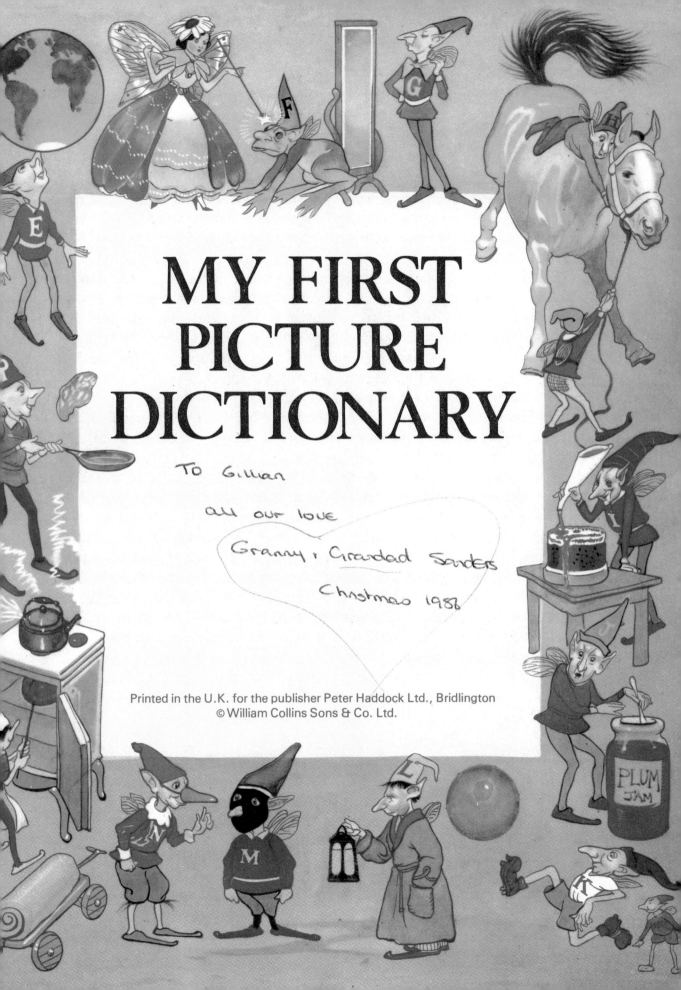

MY FIRST PICTURE DICTIONARY

To Gillian

all our love

Granny & Grandad Sanders

Christmas 1988

Printed in the U.K. for the publisher Peter Haddock Ltd., Bridlington
© William Collins Sons & Co. Ltd.

Working with My First Picture Dictionary

WORDS are the most important things in our lives. How important it is, therefore, for children to begin to understand as early as possible their meaning and application. This book aims to do just that—to help children to learn the proper use of words and to teach them the meaning of new words; to aid them in their struggle for self-expression. But the word "dictionary" is a formidable one, and only by means of a dictionary such as this, treated in an attractive and original way, can we hope to stir the young reader's interest.

My First Picture Dictionary aims to amuse while it instructs. The children's attention is first captured by the pictures, and they are then led happily to read the words describing the pictures. Without realising it, they learn, for example, that the word "fair" has many different meanings—that it can describe a colouring or the weather, etc.; and, in passing, they renew acquaintance with the familiar rhyme of Simple Simon and the pie-man going to the fair.

This is a picture-story book as well as a dictionary, and the boy or girl who reads it will find many favourite nursery characters here, and will meet Jack and Jill, the children on whose adventures the book is based. Through them they will learn, for instance, the letters of the alphabet, the days of the week, the months in the year (such items are repeated as often as possible so that they become fixed in their memory), and will absorb naturally the meanings of all the simple words within the scope of their understanding.

Emphasis has been laid on repetition, so that the young readers, having learned the meaning of a word, find it in use again and again, and so add it unconsciously to their vocabulary. Each word which is being described is emphasised when used in a sentence, and from its context in the sentence the boy or girl is led to understand its meaning, aided by picture and rhyme.

There is a liberal use of the alphabet, and its constant repetition makes it easy and familiar to the young reader.

This book will also prove of great value to parents and teachers who have difficulty in persuading children to read and to find out for themselves the meaning of words. Jack and Jill will help them over the fence!

afraid   Jill is **afraid** of the mouse. She has a fear of it.
The mouse is **afraid** of the cat. He has a fear of it.
The cat is **afraid** of the dog. He has a fear of it.

They are all **afraid**.

after

Jack runs **after** Jill. Jill
is in front of him. Jack is
behind. He is **after** her.

After Jack has chased Jill,
they will go home.
They will play again in the
afternoon. After twelve o'clock it will be **after**noon.
At noon it is twelve o'clock.

again   Dad tries to start his car. It will not start.
He tries once more. He tries **again**.
He tries often. He tries **again** and **again**.

against   Jack and Jill play tennis.
They play **against** each other. They are on opposite sides.

Dad leans **against** the wall.
The dog pushes **against** the gate.

age

How old is Jill?

Her **age** is six. It is 6.

What is Jack's **age**?

He is seven years old. His **age** is 7.

Jack is one year older than Jill.

---

air

We all breathe **air**. The birds fly in the **air**. The balloon is full of **air**. It floats in the **air**. The aeroplane flies in the **air**.

---

alive

One, two, three, four, five,
Once I caught a fish **alive**.

This fish is **alive**. It is not dead.

This fish is dead. It is not **alive**.

---

all

They **all** ran after the farmer's wife.
Every one of the Three Blind Mice ran. They **all** ran.

They ran for the whole day.
They ran **all** the day.

---

alphabet

The **alphabet** is all the letters we use.
Can you say the **alphabet**?
There are twenty-six letters in the **alphabet**.

There are 26.

ABCDEFG
HIJKLMN
OPQRSTU
VWXYZ

also

The cow has four legs.
It **also** has a tail. It has a tail, too.

always

Jack and Jill **always** try to be good.
They try to be good at all times.

an

The hen lays **an** egg. It lays one egg.

An egg.

Jill has **an** apple. She has one apple.

An apple. **An** egg and **an** apple.

angry

Jill is not happy. She is **angry**.

Jack is not **angry**. He is happy.

animals

The **animals** went in two by two,
The elephant and the kangaroo.

The elephant and the kangaroo are wild **animals**.
Some **animals** are tame. Jack's dog is a tame animal.
Some **animals** are wild. The tiger is a wild animal.

any

Jack may have **any** toy from the tree. He may choose one toy.

Does he need **any** help?
Does he need some help?
No, he does not need **any**.

---

ape

An **ape** is an animal.
It is a wild animal.
You can see an **ape** in the zoo.
Some apes live in Africa.

---

apple

An **apple** a day keeps the doctor away.

An **apple** is a fruit. It is good to eat. It is good for you. Apples grow on trees.

 Here is a green **apple**. It is not ripe.

 Here is a red **apple**. It is ripe. It is ready to eat.

April

April is the name of a month. There are twelve months.

January, February, March, **April**, May, June, July, August, September, October, November, December.

---

arm

The tin soldier has lost its **arm.** It has one **arm** on, and one **arm** off.

Jack has two arms.

arrow   Jack has a bow and **arrow**. The **arrow** is a stick with a point at one end. Jack puts the **arrow** in the bow. Then he shoots the **arrow** into the air.

as   Mary had a little lamb.
Its fleece was white **as** snow.

Its fleece was like the colour of snow.
It was **as** white **as** snow.

asleep

Where is the boy who looks after the sheep?
He's under a haystack, fast **asleep**.

Little Boy Blue is sleepy. He is not awake. He has gone to sleep. He is **asleep**.

August   **August** is the name of a month. There are twelve months in a year.

January   February   March   April   May   June   July
August   September   October   November   December

aunt   Jack and Jill have an **aunt**.
She is **Aunt** May.
Aunt May is Dad's sister.
They have another **aunt**.
She is **Aunt** Jane.
Aunt Jane is Mother's sister.

B b *b*

baa

Baa, baa, black sheep.
Have you any wool?

Baa is the cry of a sheep.
Moo is the cry of a cow.
Some sheep are black.
Some sheep are white.

baby

A **baby** is a small child. There is
one **baby** at one end of the pram,
and one **baby** at the other end.
There are two babies in the pram.

back

Jill has her **back** to the wall.
Her **back** is against the wall.
It is the **back** of her body.
She has come **back** from a ride.

She rode on her pony's **back**.
She has been out. Now she is **back**.

bad   Jack is not a good boy. He is **bad**.
He went out in the rain. It was **bad** for him.
He may get a **bad** cold. It was a **bad** day.

---

bag      Dad has a golf-**bag**.
Mother has a shopping-**bag**.
Jill has a **bag** of sweets.

---

bake   Pat-a-cake, pat-a-cake, baker's man,
Bake me a cake as fast as you can.

To **bake** is to cook in the oven.

---

ball   Jack has a **ball**. It is red.
Jill has a **ball**. It is blue.
There are two balls.

When they are big, Jack and Jill will go
to a **ball**. They will dance at the **ball**.

---

banana   A **banana** is a fruit. It has a yellow skin.
Peel off the yellow skin before you eat the **banana**.

bank

Here is Jack's **bank**. He puts his coins in it.

Here is Dad's **bank**. He keeps his money in it. The man who looks after the **bank** is called the banker.

Here is the **bank** of a river. It is the ground at the edge of the river.

---

bark

Hark! hark! The dogs do **bark**.

A dog says, "Bow-wow!" It gives a **bark**. It is barking. A tree wears a coat to keep warm. It is called the **bark**. The dog can **bark**. The tree wears a **bark**.

---

barrel

Here is a big **barrel**.
The big **barrel** is red.

Here is a little **barrel**.
The little **barrel** is blue.

---

barrow

Dad has a **barrow** in the garden. The **barrow** has one wheel. Dad wheels his **barrow**. It is a wheel**barrow**.

bat

Jack plays cricket with the boy next door. The boy is called Tom.

Tom throws the ball. Jack hits it with his **bat**.

Here is another **bat**. It flies, but it is not a bird. It is like a mouse with wings.

bath

The **bath** is in the **bath**room. Jill puts water in the **bath**. The water comes from the taps.
Jill has a **bath**. She washes herself in the **bath**. Then she is clean.

beach

Jack and Jill are at the seaside. They are on the **beach**. It is the sandy part at the side of the sea.

They are building a castle on the **beach**. It is made from sand from the **beach**.

bear

A **bear** is a wild animal. It has thick fur. You can see a **bear** in the zoo. Jill has a teddy-**bear**.

beard

Each of the Seven Dwarfs has a **beard**. Each has hair on his face.

Dad has no **beard**. He shaves off the hair every day.

beast

Beast is another name for an animal.
Some beasts are wild. Some beasts are tame.
The cow is a tame **beast**. The tiger is a wild **beast**.
The zoo is full of beasts.
Can you tell which are tame beasts, and which are wild beasts ?

beat

The man in the band will **beat** the drum.
He will hit the drum.

Jack **beat** Jill. He ran much
faster than Jill. He **beat** her.
He could feel his heart **beat**.

because

Dad is now a man **because**
he grew up. He is a man, for
the reason that he grew up.

bed

Sleepy-head ! It's time for **bed**.

How many legs has a **bed** ?
A **bed** has as many legs as a cow has.

bee

A **bee** is an insect. It makes a noise like buzz-buzz. It is buzzing.
A **bee** makes honey from the flowers. It lives in a hive. It works hard. When you are busy, you are as busy as a **bee**.

before

Look **before** you leap.
Look earlier than you leap.

Jill is **before** Jack. She is in front of him. She will leap **before** him. She will leap earlier than him.

beg

Jack's dog can **beg**.
It begs for a bone.
Jill's cat can **beg**.
It begs for milk.

The cat and dog have begged.
They have been begging.

behind

The horse is in front.
The cart is **behind**.
The horse is before the cart.
The cart is **behind** the horse.

believe

Do you **believe** in fairies? Do you think there are fairies? Yes, I think there are fairies.
I **believe** that there are fairies.

bell

Ding, dong, **bell**,
Pussy's in the well.

A **bell** rings. Jack rings
the **bell** on his bicycle.

When he comes home he rings the **bell** on the door. It is
the door**bell.** On Sunday the church **bell** rings.

---

below

Dad's head is **below** his hat. His hat is on top. It is above.
His head is **below**. It is under his hat.

---

belt

Jill wears a **belt** on her frock.
Where does she wear the **belt**?
She wears the **belt** round her waist.

---

beneath

The stars are in the sky.
We are **beneath** the sky. We are under the sky.

---

berry

A **berry** is a small fruit with seeds in it.

This is a goose**berry**.

This is a straw**berry**.

This is a rasp**berry**.

Jack and Jill like to pick berries from the bushes. They like
to eat them.

beside

Jill goes to school with Pat, who lives next door.
Jill walks to school **beside** Pat.
They walk side by side.
Jill sits **beside** Pat at school.
They sit side by side.

best

Pat can read well. But Jill can read **best** of all. No one at school can read as well as Jill. She is the **best**.
Jill likes to read and to count. But she likes to play **best**. She likes to play most of all.

between

Jack walks **between** Mother and Dad. He has someone on each side of him. He is **between**.

bicycle

Jack rides his **bicycle**. If he falls off, he will have had an accident.

big

The elephant is **big**. It is very large.
The mouse is little. It is not **big**.
A **big** elephant.
A little mouse.

bird

A **bird** has feathers. A **bird** has wings.
Most birds can fly.

Here is a big **bird**. It is an eagle.

Here is a little **bird**. It is a robin.

Here is a pet **bird**. It is in a cage.
It can speak. It is a parrot.

birthday

Jill's **birthday** is on the third of April.
That is the day when she was born.
On the third of April Jill has a party.
It is her **birthday** party.
She is six. She is 6.
She has six candles on her
birthday cake. She has 6.

bit

Jill took a **bit** of birthday cake. She took a piece of cake.
She **bit** it. She began to eat it.

bite

When Jill bit the cake, she took a **bite** of cake.

black

Black is a colour. Coal is **black**.
Here is a **black** bird.

This is **black**.

blood

Jack has cut his hand.
There is **blood** on it. **Blood** is red.
We all have **blood** in our bodies.

blow

Jack will **blow** up his balloon. He will put air into it.
He will hit the balloon. He will give it a **blow**.

blue

Blue is a colour. Jill has a **blue** frock.

 This is **blue**.

boat

The owl and the pussy-cat went to sea,
In a beautiful pea-green **boat**.

A **boat** can carry you over the
water. You can row a **boat**.
A big **boat** is called a ship.

body

Jack has a **body**. Jill has a **body**. Animals have bodies.
We all have bodies. Every part of you together is your **body**.

bone

Old Mother Hubbard went to the cupboard
To get her poor dog a **bone**.

We all have bones in our bodies.
A **bone** is hard.

boot

This is a **boot**.

This is a shoe.

---

born

Jill was **born** on the third of April. That is her birthday.

Here is a new puppy.
It was **born** today.
Today is its birthday.

---

bow

Jack has a **bow**. He puts an arrow in it. He shoots with his **bow**.

Jill has a **bow**. It is made of ribbon. She ties the **bow** on her hair.

Jack makes a **bow**. He bends his head down, and bows.

---

box

The matches are in a **box**. A **box** of matches.
Jack keeps his toys in a big **box**. The **box** is made of wood.
Jack and Tom **box** each other. They are boxing.

---

boy

When Jack was born he was a baby.
Now he is a **boy**.
When he grows up, he will be a man.

bread

The baker bakes **bread**. He puts it in the oven. It is made of flour. We cut **bread** from a loaf. A loaf of **bread**. We eat it. We put butter or jam on the **bread**.

break

The cup fell off the table. Did the cup **break**? Yes, it broke into pieces. The cup was broken.

breakfast

Jack and Jill have porridge for **breakfast**. Then they go to school. **Breakfast** is the first meal of the day.

breath

Take a deep **breath** before you begin to run. Fill your lungs with air.
Blow your **breath** into the balloon to blow it up.

bricks

Jill has toy **bricks**. She builds a house with them. You can see the alphabet on her **bricks**.

Dad builds a wall with big **bricks**. There is no alphabet on his **bricks**.

bride

Here comes the **bride** !
The fairy princess is the **bride**.
She has married the fairy prince.
Mother was Dad's **bride**.

bring

Leave them alone, and they'll come home,
And **bring** their tails behind them.

Bring the book to me. Carry the book to me.

brother

Jack is Jill's **brother**. Jill is Jack's sister.
Jack and Jill have the same father and mother.
Jack and Jill are **brother** and sister.

brown

Brown is a colour. The teddy-bear is **brown**.

This is **brown**.

brush

Jill has a hair**brush** to **brush** her hair.
She has a tooth**brush** to **brush** her teeth.
She has a paint**brush** to paint her pictures.

The fox has a bushy tail.
It is called a **brush**.

build

Jill can **build** with her bricks.
Dad can **build** with his big bricks.

bunch

This flower is by itself.   These flowers are in a **bunch**.

burn

The fire is not lit. Mother puts a match to the fire to light it. Then the fire will **burn**. It will **burn** wood and sticks. Do not play with matches. You may **burn** your fingers. A **burn** will hurt. It will give you pain.

bus

Mother goes to shop in a **bus**.
It is a big motor car.
The **bus** has many seats in it.

busy

As **busy** as a bee.
A bee is very **busy**. It works hard. It is **busy** making honey.

but

Jill is on her pony. There is no one on the pony **but** Jill. There is no one except Jill on the pony.
The pony can run, **but** it cannot jump.

butcher

A **butcher** is a man who sells meat. He keeps a shop. It is called a **butcher's** shop.

butter

We get milk from the cow. We make **butter** from the milk. We eat bread and **butter**.

---

butterfly

> A **butterfly**
> Can flutter by.

A **butterfly** has four wings. It has lovely colours on its wings. It is like a flying flower.

---

buy

Jack has five pence. He is going to **buy** some sweets. He will pay 5p to **buy** a bag of sweets.

---

by

Jack stands **by** Jill. He is beside Jill.
They watch the trains go **by**.
They watch the trains go past them.

They must be home **by** tea-time. They must be home not later than tea-time.

C C *c*

cage

The monkeys are in a **cage** at the zoo. They are in a big **cage**.

Jack has a bird in a **cage**. It is in a little **cage**.

cake

There were six candles on Jill's birthday **cake**. Jill ate a bit of her birthday **cake**.

Mother baked the **cake** in the oven.

calf

Here is a **calf**.
It is a cow's baby.

Here is a cow.
It is the mother of the **calf**.

call

What do they **call** you?
They **call** me Jill.
My name is Jill.

Pat will **call** on Jill.
She will visit Jill.

camel

A **camel** is a big animal.
It has one hump or two humps on its back.
There is a **camel** at the zoo. You can ride on the **camel**.

candle

Jill had six candles on her birthday cake.
Mother lit each **candle** with a match.

car

Jack has a toy **car**.

Dad has a real **car**. It has four wheels.

Jack and Jill go for a ride in a **car**. It goes very fast.

care

Take **care** when you cross the street. Be careful. Be full of **care**.
Jack and Jill **care** for their pets. They look after them.
They do not **care** for rice. They do not like to eat rice.

carry

Jill can **carry** her cat. She lifts it in her arms and carries it.

cat

Jill calls her **cat** Pussy.
A baby **cat** is called a kitten.

---

catch

Throw the ball to Jack and he will **catch** it in his hand.

Run after the dog and **catch** it. Take hold of it.

Do not go out in the rain, or you will **catch** cold. You will get cold.

---

chase

Dad is going to **chase** his hat.
He is going to run after his hat.

He is chasing the hat. The hat is being chased.

---

cheese

We get milk from the cow. We get cream from the milk. We make butter from the cream. We also make **cheese** from the cream. We eat **cheese**.

---

cherry

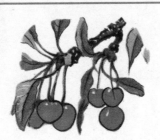

A **cherry** grows on a tree.
It is a fruit.
Cherries are good to eat.

children
There was an old woman who lived in a shoe.
She had so many **children** she didn't know what to do.

The old woman had many boys and girls to look after.

---

chill
The wind is **chill**. It is a cold wind. It is a chilly day.

Jill is in bed with a cold.
She has caught a **chill**.

---

chimney

Santa Claus comes down the **chimney**.

The **chimney** is above the roof. It lets the smoke out from the fire.

Christmas
Christmas Day is the birthday of Jesus. It is the 25th of December.

Jack and Jill hang up their stockings on **Christmas** Eve. On **Christmas** Day they find presents in them.

They have a **Christmas** tree.

They have a merry **Christmas**.

circus

At Christmas Aunt Jane took Jack and Jill to the **circus**. The **circus** was in a big tent. The animals did tricks. The elephants danced. The horses ran round the ring. A man cracked his whip. The clown played pranks. Jack and Jill had great fun at the **circus**.

class

Jill and Pat are in the same **class** at school. There are twenty girls in the **class**. There are 20.

They are all at the same stage. They are all in the one **class**.

claws

A cat has **claws** on each foot. It has four feet. It has 4.

A bird has **claws** on each foot. It has two feet. It has 2.

clean

When Jack plays with clay, his hands are not **clean**. They are dirty.

He will wash himself.
Then he will be **clean**.

He will **clean** himself.

clever

At the circus an elephant stood on its head.
It was a **clever** trick.

The elephant was **clever** to learn such a trick.
It used its brains.

---

climb

When we **climb** the stairs, we go up the stairs.
When we **climb** a hill, we go up a hill.
Jack likes to **climb** trees. He likes climbing.

---

clock

Hickory, dickory, dock,
The mouse ran up the **clock**.

A **clock** tells you the time.
It ticks off the minutes and the hours.

Big Ben is a big **clock** in London.

---

cloth

Jill's coat is made of **cloth**. Her dress is made of **cloth**.
All her clothes are made of **cloth**.

---

clothes

The maid was in the garden hanging out the **clothes**
When by came a blackbird and snapped off her nose.

The maid hangs out the **clothes**. They are made of cloth.

clown   Jack and Jill saw a **clown** at the circus.
He was a funny man.
He did funny tricks.

coal   What do you burn on the fire?
We burn **coal**.

Coal is black. **Coal** comes out of the ground.
It is deep down under the earth. It is in a **coal** mine.

coat   Jill is going out. She puts on her **coat**.
A bear has a **coat**. It is made of fur.
A bird has a **coat**. It is made of feathers.
A tree has a **coat**. It is made of bark.
Jill's **coat** is made of cloth.

cold   Jill puts on her coat, because it is a **cold** day. The coat will
keep her warm. If she has no coat, she may catch a **cold**.
She will feel **cold**. Then she will be ill.

collar   Jack's dog wears a **collar** round its neck.

Jack has a **collar** on his shirt.

Jill has a **collar** at the neck of her dress.

colour

A cabbage is green.
Green is its **colour**.

A cherry is red.
Red is its **colour**.

There are many colours in Jack's paint-box. He can **colour** pictures with his paints. He can use green, blue, yellow, red, white and black.

What **colour** is snow?

---

come

There were two blackbirds sitting on a hill,
The one named Jack, the other named Jill.
Fly away, Jack! Fly away, Jill!
Come again, Jack! **Come** again, Jill!

" **Come** to me, Pussy," cries Jill. Her cat comes to her. It does not run away. It has **come** to her.

---

copy

Jill has two dolls.
They are called Milly and Molly.
They are both alike.
They are twin dolls.
Milly is a **copy** of Molly.
Molly is a **copy** of Milly.

Jill can **copy** the pictures in her story book.

---

corner

Little Jack Horner
Sat in a **corner**.

cottage

Little Red Riding Hood went to visit her Granny.

Her Granny lived in a **cottage** in the wood.

A **cottage** is a small house.

---

count

Can you **count** up to ten?
Ten little pigs went to market.

One	two	three	four	five	six	seven	eight	nine	ten
1	2	3	4	5	6	7	8	9	10

---

country

The farmer lives in the **country**. He does not live in the town.

There are no shops and streets in the **country**. There are green fields and trees.

The **country** we live in is called Britain.

---

cow

Hey, diddle, diddle,
The cat and the fiddle,
The **cow** jumped over the moon.

The **cow** eats grass.
It gives milk and cream.
We make butter and cheese from cream.

A **cow** has four legs.

crash
Jack bumped into the wall on his bicycle. There was a **crash**.

The bicycle crashed into the wall. He had an accident.

---

cricket
Jack and Tom play **cricket**.
They play with a **cricket** ball and a **cricket** bat.

---

cross
Jack was **cross** when he fell off his bicycle. He was angry.

Cross the bridge to get to the other side of the river.
Go across the bridge.

This is a red **cross**.

---

crow
Early in the morning you can hear the cock **crow**.
" Cock-a-doodle-doo ! " he crows.

A **crow** is a big black bird.
The **crow** says, " Caw-caw ! "

---

crowd
There were many boys and girls at Jill's party.
There was a **crowd** of children.

They had to **crowd** into the house. There was not much room for them.
They had to keep close together. They were crowded.

crown

The Queen wears a crown on her head. It is like a hat. There are jewels in the **crown**.

---

cry

Jack gave a **cry** when he fell off his bicycle. He gave a shout.
Jill began to **cry**. Tears fell from her eyes.
She was crying. She cried.

---

cup

Mother puts four cups on the table at tea-time.

There is one **cup** for Dad.
There is one **cup** for Mother.
There is one **cup** for Jack.
There is one **cup** for Jill.

There are 4 cups.

---

curl

There was a little girl,
And she had a little **curl**.

Jill's hair can **curl**. It is curly.
Pussy likes to **curl** up on the rug.

---

cut

Mother has **cut** the bread with a knife.

Jill has **cut** out pictures with a pair of scissors.

Jack has **cut** his finger on a piece of glass.

D d *d*

Dad

Dad is Jack and Jill's father.
His name is Mr. Brown. But Jack and Jill call him **Dad**.

---

dairy

A **dairy** is a place where milk and cream are kept. Butter and cheese are made in the **dairy**.

---

daisy

A **daisy** is a flower. It grows wild in the fields. It is white or pink, with a yellow heart.
Jill likes to make a **daisy**-chain.

---

dance

Mother plays the piano, and Jack and Jill **dance**. They hop about on their toes. They keep time to the music.

danger

Oh dear! Pussy is in **danger**.
She is on the roof.
How will she get down?
It is a dangerous place.

---

date

The **date** of Jill's birthday
is the third of April.
What **date** is it today?
Look at the calendar and you will see.

A **date** is the day of the month,
the month itself, and the year.
A different kind of **date** is a fruit.
It grows on a big tree called a
date palm.

---

daughter Jill is the **daughter** of Dad and Mother. Jack is the son.

---

day

Through the **day** it is light. At night it is dark. The light
and the dark together make one **day**.
There are twenty-four hours in a **day**. There are 24.

---

dead

These flowers are alive.

These flowers are **dead**.

deaf
Granny is an old lady.
She cannot hear well.
She is **deaf**.
We have to shout in her ear.

December
December is the name of a month. It is the last month in the year. Christmas Day is in **December**. The date is the twenty-fifth of **December**.

---

deed
A Scout does a good **deed** every day. He does a good thing every day.

---

deer
Bambi is a **deer**.

---

dentist
The **dentist** keeps Jack and Jill's teeth in order. They like to take care of their teeth. The **dentist** helps them.

---

desk

A **desk** is a kind of table.
Jill sits at a **desk** at school.
Dad works at a **desk** in his office.

dictionary   This book is a **dictionary**. A **dictionary** tells you the meanings of words. The words in the **dictionary** are in the order of the alphabet.

All the words that begin with A are together. All the words with B are together. Can you tell what letter the word " clown " is under ?

die   The man will cut down the tree. The tree is alive. When it is cut down, it will be dead. The tree will **die**.

different   A cat and a cow are not alike. They are **different**. They are not the same. What is **different** about them ? Can you tell the difference ?

dinner

Dinner is the main meal of the day. What do you like to eat for **dinner** ? I like soup. I like meat and vegetables. I like apple-pie.

dish   The **dish** ran away with the spoon.

We eat food from a **dish**. We keep dishes in the cupboard.

divide

Here is a whole apple.
Divide the apple into parts.

The apple is not whole.
It has been divided.

---

doctor

Doctor, doctor! Please be quick.
Jack's in bed. He's feeling sick.

Jack is ill. The **doctor** will come and help him to get well.

---

dog

The little **dog** laughed
To see such fun.

The **dog** barks. It says, " Bow-wow."
Jack's **dog** can sit up and beg.

---

doll

Jill has one **doll** called Milly, and one **doll** called Molly.
They are both alike. They are twins.
Jill takes the dolls for a walk. She puts them to bed at night.

---

donkey

There is a **donkey** at the farm.
When Jack goes to the farm, he
has a ride on the **donkey**.
The **donkey** has long ears.
It says, " Hee-haw ! "

---

door

Open the **door** and come in. There is a **door** on the house.
It is the outside **door**. There are doors in all the rooms.
There is a **door** on the cupboard. Open the **door**, or shut
the **door**.

down The clock struck one.
The mouse ran **down**.
Hickory, dickory, dock.

The mouse ran up the clock to a high place.
Then the mouse ran **down** to a low place.

---

downstairs When we go up the stairs, we go upstairs.
When we go down the stairs, we go **downstairs**.

---

dozen A **dozen** is twelve. It is 12.
Jack has a **dozen** tin soldiers. He has twelve. He has 12.

---

draw The horse will **draw** the cart. It will pull the cart.
Jack can **draw** a picture. He likes
drawing. When he has drawn the
picture he will paint it.

---

dress Jill can **dress** her dolls.

Milly has a blue **dress**.

Molly has a red **dress**.

Jill has a yellow **dress**.

drink

If all the world were apple-pie,
And all the seas were ink ;
If all the trees were bread and cheese,
What should we have to **drink** ?

Pussy likes to **drink** milk.
The dog likes a **drink** of water.
Jill drank a cup of tea. She likes drinking tea.

---

drive

Dad can **drive** the car. He takes Jack and Jill for a **drive**.
He is the driver.

They have been driven to the sea before. Dad drove them.
Some hens run on to the road. They **drive** the hens away.
They chase them away.

---

drop

A **drop** of rain falls.
You can see it **drop** down from the sky.

---

drown

A boy fell into the river. Dad pulled him out. The boy was
going to **drown**. He was under the water. He would die
because he could not get air. He was drowning.

drum   The man in the band played a **drum**.
"Rub-a-dub-dub!" says the **drum**.

---

dry

Jill washes her face. It is wet.
She will **dry** it with a towel.
Then it will be **dry**.
She hangs out her doll's clothes
to **dry**.

---

duck   A **duck** says, "Quack-quack."
A **duck** is a bird. It can swim. Some ducks can fly.

E e *e*

each

Each little pig has a curly tail.
Every one of the three pigs has a
curly tail.

eagle

The **eagle** is a big bird. It lives high up in the hills.

ear

Jill has one **ear** on one side of
her head. She has one **ear** on the
other side.
She has two ears. She has one on
each side.

She can hear with her ears.

early

Early to bed, **early** to rise,
Makes a man healthy, wealthy and wise.

The cock crows **early** in the morning.
He crows before anyone else is awake.
He is an **early** bird.

The **early** bird catches the worm.

earn

Dad goes to work to **earn** money.
He is paid for his work. He earns money.

earth

We all live on the **earth**. It is the world.
The **earth** is round.

Dad digs in the garden. He digs the **earth** in the garden.

east

There are four points of the earth.
They are north, south, **east**, west.

The sun rises in the **east**.

eat

The Queen was in the parlour
Eating bread and honey.

The Queen begins to **eat** her bread and honey.
She is eating it. Soon she will have eaten it all.

egg

Higgledy, piggledy, my black hen.
She lays eggs for gentlemen.
Sometimes nine, and sometimes ten,
Higgledy, piggledy, my black hen.

Jill eats an **egg** for breakfast.
The hen lays the **egg** in a nest.
Sometimes Jill eats a boiled **egg**.

E e e

eight

Eight is a number.

1   2   3   4   5   6   7   **8**
One   two   three   four   five   six   seven   **eight.**

There are **eight** chickens in a row. Can you count them?

either

What would you like to eat?
You may have an apple or an orange.
You may have one or the other.
You may have **either** an apple or an orange.

elephant

The **elephant** is a big animal. It has a long trunk. It has funny ears. It has a short tail.

The **elephant** tried to jump through a hoop at the circus.

eleven

Eleven is a number. Can you count up to **eleven**?

One two three four five six seven eight nine ten **eleven**
1   2   3   4   5   6   7   8   9   10   **11**

empty

One glass is full of milk.
One glass is **empty**.
There is nothing in the **empty** glass.

England
England is a country.
The boys and girls in **England**
speak English.
They are English children.
This book is written in English.
Here is a map of **England**
where the English live.

envelope
Put the letter in an **envelope**.
Write the address on the **envelope**.
Stick a stamp on the **envelope**.
Give the **envelope** to the postman.

equal
Two one pound coins are **equal**.
They have the same value.
Fifty pence and a pound are not **equal**. They are different.
One pound is **equal** to a hundred pence.
It is the same in value as a hundred pence.

even

Even a cat may look at a king.
Anybody may look at a king;
even a cat.

The road is bumpy. It is not **even**.

Jack and Tom ran a race. They were **even** at the end of
the race. They both finished at the same time.

evening
At the beginning of the day it is morning.
At the end of the day it is **evening**.

every   Every day the sun rises in the east.
The sun rises in the east each day.

everywhere   Jill has lost Pussy.
She has looked **everywhere**.
She has looked in every place.
Can you see Pussy?

except   Jill looked everywhere for Pussy, **except** under the table.
She looked in every place, but not under the table.

excuse   Uncle Jack could not come to the circus.
He sent an **excuse**.
His **excuse** was that he was too busy.
He wrote, " Please **excuse** me." He meant, " Please for-give me."

eye

Who saw him die?
" I," said the Fly,
" With my little **eye**,
I saw him die."

Jack has two eyes. He sees with his eyes.
All beasts and birds have eyes.

Oh, my! There is a fly in Jack's **eye**.

F f _f_

face

Jack and Jill are going to dance.
They **face** each other. They are **face** to **face**.

Jill looks in the mirror to see her **face**.
She is facing the mirror.

fair

You must not cheat when you play a game.
It is not **fair**. You must play **fair**.

Mother has **fair** hair. It is light.
Dad has black hair. His hair is not **fair**.

Simple Simon met a pie-man
Going to the **fair**.

Jack and Jill went to a **fair**. What fun they had at the **fair**!
The day was **fair**. It was not raining.

fairy

Here is the **Fairy** Queen.

Jill likes to read **fairy** stories. She believes in fairies.

---

family

The Browns are a **family**.
Dad, Mother, Jack and Jill are the **family**.

---

far

Over the hills and **far** away.
The aeroplane is flying **far** away.
It is flying a long way.

How **far** is it to school?
How **far** away is school?

---

farm

Uncle Jack lives on a **farm**. He is a farmer. He has sheep and cows on his **farm**. He grows corn and hay on the **farm**. He has a barn on the **farm**.

---

fat

To market, to market, to buy a **fat** pig,
Home again, home again, jiggety-jig.

Here is a **fat** pig.

Here is a thin pig.

father

Mr. Brown is Jack and Jill's **father**.
They call him Dad.
He is married to Mother.

---

fear

The mouse is afraid of the cat.
It feels **fear**.
It fears the cat.

February

February is the name of a month.
There are twelve months in a year. There are 12.

January	**February**	March	April	May	June	July
1	2	3	4	5	6	7

August	September	October	November	December
8	9	10	11	12

---

feed

Feed the birds in winter.
Give them some food to eat. You will be feeding the birds.
Then they will be fed.

---

fence

Jack's pony jumps over the **fence**.
Uncle Jack has many fences on his
farm. They keep the animals safe
in the fields.

---

few

Have you any sweets?
I have only a **few** left. There are not many.
There are one or two. There are a **few**.

F f

field

There is a big **field** on Uncle Jack's farm. The sheep and cows are in the **field**.

There are other fields on the farm, too. There is corn in one **field**, and hay in another.

figure

What is the **figure** four? 4 is the **figure** four. Numbers are figures. 1 2 3 4 5 6 7 8 9 10. These are the figures from one to ten.

Jack can draw the **figure** of a man. He can draw the shape of a man.

find

Jack and Jill play hide-and-seek. Jack hides, and Jill has to **find** him. She looks everywhere till she finds him. Then she has found him.

finger

Mother wears a ring on her **finger**. We have five fingers on the left hand. We have five fingers on the right hand. We have ten fingers. We have 10.

fire

The **fire** burns in the **fire**place. It burns sticks and coals. It keeps us warm. Do not go too near the **fire**. You may burn yourself.

Jack can **fire** his gun. He shoots when he fires.

first

If at **first** you don't succeed,
Try, try, try again !

Jack won a race. He was **first**. Nobody was in front of him.

Jack's birthday is on the **first** of March.
It is on the **first** day of March.

Wash your hands **first,** and then have tea.

fish

A **fish** lives in water.
There are many fishes in the sea.

We eat **fish**.

Jack keeps gold**fish** in a bowl.

Dad goes to **fish** in a river.
He is fishing.

fit

Try on your shoes to see if they will **fit**.
Find out if they are the right size.
Will your feet **fit** into your shoes ?

five

You have **five** fingers on each hand.
You have 5 fingers.

You have **five** toes on each foot.
You have 5 toes.

One	two	three	four	**five**
1	2	3	4	**5**

flag

Every country has its own **flag**.

The **flag** of Great Britain is called the Union Jack.

The **flag** of America is called the Stars and Stripes.
Ships have flags.

---

float

Jack's toy boat will **float** on the water. It will not sink. It floats.

Jack can lie flat on his back and **float** on the water.

---

flower

Roses are red,
Violets are blue.
Sugar is sweet
And so are you !

What **flower** do you like best ? Do you like roses, lilies, pansies, daisies, or buttercups ?

Some flowers grow in the fields. They are wild flowers.

---

fly

Birds travel through the air with their wings. They **fly**.
They are flying. They have flown away.

An aeroplane can **fly**.
The aeroplane flew away.

" Will you walk into my parlour ? "
Said the spider to the **fly**.

food

Food is what we eat. We chew our **food**. Then we swallow it.

We need **food** to make us grow. **Food** keeps us well and strong.

We give animals **food**. We feed them.

---

foot

Jack has one left **foot** and one right **foot**. He has two feet. He wears socks and shoes on his feet.

---

football

Dad goes to see a **football** match. It is played by a **football** team. They play with a **football**. They kick it with their feet.

---

for

Old King Cole
Was a merry old soul,
And a merry old soul was he.
He called **for** his pipe,
He called **for** his bowl,
And he called **for** his fiddlers three.

What do you want **for** Christmas?
I asked Santa Claus **for** a toy train **for** Christmas.

Jill ran **for** her cat. She ran to fetch her cat.

Jack uses an orange **for** a ball.
He uses it in place of a ball.

forest

A **forest** is a big wood.
There are many trees in a **forest**.

The Seven Dwarfs lived in a little
house in the **forest**.

forget

Dad came back for his hat. He forgot it. Why did he **forget**
his hat? He did not remember to take it with him. He had
forgotten it. He will not **forget** it again.

fork

We use a knife and **fork** when we eat. We
cut our food with a knife. We lift the
food to our mouth with the **fork**.
A fork has prongs on it.

four

Four little dolls, as you can see,
Sat down to have a cup of tea.

How many dolls had tea? There were **four** dolls. There
were 4.

Two and two make **four**.
Jack has two apples. Jill has two apples.
They have **four** apples.

One	two	three	**four**
1	2	3	4

fox

A **fox** is a wild animal.
It is a member of the dog family.

It has a bushy tail called a brush.

The **fox** is very clever and cunning.

freeze   It is very cold. The water will **freeze**. There will be ice on the water. The water will be frozen. It has been freezing.

Friday   **Friday** is the sixth day of the week.
Sunday Monday Tuesday Wednesday Thursday **Friday** Saturday.

fruit   What **fruit** do you like best to eat ?
Do you like apples, pears, oranges, grapes, bananas, or plums ?

Fruit grows on trees and bushes.

full   Yes, sir ! Yes, sir !
Three bags **full**.

The bags are **full**. The bags cannot hold any more. They are filled up. When the bags are not **full**, you can put more inside them.

fur   Some animals have soft hair on their skin. It is **fur**. **Fur** keeps them warm. Mother has a **fur** coat.

G g g

game

Cricket is a **game**. Hide-and-seek is a **game**.
Football is a **game**. Jack and Jill like to play games.

gander

Goosey, goosey **gander**,
Whither shall I wander?

A **gander** is a male goose.

garage

Dad keeps his car in a **garage**.
It is a kind of house for his car.
He garages his car.

garden

Dad grows flowers and fruit and vegetables in the **garden**.
He digs in the **garden**. He plants seeds in the **garden**. He
is gardening. A man who works in a **garden** is called a
gardener.

gate

The farmer opens the **gate** in the field to let the sheep out.
He shuts the **gate** to keep the sheep in.

giant

The little man is a dwarf.
The big man is a **giant**.
Jill read about giants in her
fairy stories.

giraffe

A **giraffe** is a wild animal. You
can see a **giraffe** at the zoo. The
giraffe has four long legs and a
long neck. He feeds from leaves
high up on the trees. He can
stretch up with his long neck.

girl

Two little girls are better than one.
Two little boys can double the fun.

Jill and Pat are two little girls.
Jill is one **girl**. Pat is one **girl**. They are two girls.

give

Little Tommy Tucker
Sang for his supper.
What shall we **give** him?
Brown bread and butter.

Jack gave Jill a book for her birthday. He has given her a
gift. Next year he will be giving her a rubber ball.

glad

Pussy is **glad** when Jill plays with her.
Pussy is happy. She is not sad. She is full of gladness.

glass The window is made of **glass**. We can see through **glass**. Jack drinks a **glass** of milk for supper.

Granny wears glasses.
They are made of **glass**.
They help her to see things better.

---

go " Where are you going to, my pretty maid ? "
" I'm going a-milking, sir," she said.

The maid is going to **go** and milk the cow.

Will you **go** to school today ? Which way will you **go**? I shall **go** by bus. The bus has gone. It is not here. It went away.

---

gold Mother's ring is made of **gold**. It is golden.
Gold is a metal. Its colour is bright yellow.

---

goldfish Jack has five **goldfish** in a bowl.
They are the colour of gold.
They are like golden fish.

---

good Jill is not a bad girl. She is **good**. She does what she is told. She is fond of sweets. They are **good** to eat.

good-bye

The train is leaving.
Aunt Jane is going away.
Wave to her.
" **Good-bye**, Aunt Jane."

---

good-night   Good-night! It is time to go to bed.

> When Little Fred
> Was called to bed,
> He always acted right.
> He kissed Mama,
> And then Papa,
> And wished them all **good-night**.

---

goose

A **goose** lays an egg. A male **goose** is a gander. A crowd of geese is called a flock of geese.

---

grand

The hills looked big and **grand**. We had a **grand** view of them.
Jack and Jill had a **grand** time at the party. They had a good time. They looked very **grand** in their party clothes.

---

grape

A **grape** is a fruit.
Grapes grow in bunches.
They grow on **grape** vines.

grapefruit Grapefruit is a big yellow fruit.
We eat **grapefruit**. It grows on trees.

---

grass Grass grows on the ground. It is green.
Cows eat **grass**. Horses eat **grass**.
The farmer cuts the long **grass**, and makes it into hay.

---

great There was a **great** number of people at the zoo. There were very many people. They were watching the elephant. The elephant is a **great** animal. It is a very big animal. King Arthur was a great man. He was a good and wise man.

---

green Green is a colour. Grass is **green**. Leaves are **green**.

 This is **green**.

---

grow

Mary, Mary, quite contrary,
How does your garden **grow**?

Dad plants seeds in the ground.
They **grow** into flowers and plants.

Jack grows bigger every year.
When he was two, he was very small.
He grew bigger. He is still growing.
Dad is grown up.

growl

Spot is Jack's dog. When Spot is angry, he makes a noise. It is a **growl**. Can you hear Spot growling?

---

guess

Old Mother Twitchett had but one eye,
And a long tail which she let fly;
And every time she went over a gap,
She left a bit of her tail in a trap.

Who is Old Mother Twitchett? Can you **guess**?
Can you think of the right answer?
Old Mother Twitchett is a needle and thread.
Did you **guess** the answer?

---

guest

Jill is going to stay at Uncle Jack's farm. She will be a **guest**. A **guest** is someone who comes for a visit.

---

gun

There was a little man,
And he had a little **gun**.
And his bullets were made of lead, lead, lead.
He shot Johnny Sprig
Through the middle of his wig,
And knocked it right off his head, head, head.

H h *h*

---

had

Jill **had** a teddy-bear.
It was Jill's teddy-bear.
Jill owned it.
Jill **had** Teddy in her arms.
She held Teddy.
Has Teddy **had** tea?
Yes, Teddy has **had** tea.

---

hair

Jack and Jill get their **hair** cut.
It grows on their heads.
Mother has long **hair**.
Dad shaves off the **hair** on his face.
He has no beard.
The Dwarfs have beards.
Mother combs her **hair**.

---

half

There is only one cake left. Jack wants
a bit. Jill wants a bit. Mother must
cut it in **half**.
Mother cuts it through the middle. It
is in two equal parts.
She gives one **half** to Jack, and one
half to Jill. She has halved it.

hand

Jill has one left **hand**. She has one right **hand**. She has two hands.

She can pick things up with her hands. She can hold things in her hands. She can **hand** things to people with her hands.

She is **hand**-in-**hand** with Mother.

hang

Hang up your coat.
Are you hanging it up?
Yes, it is hung up.

Apples **hang** on trees.

Pictures **hang** on walls.

happy

The children are **happy**.
They are **happy** because
it is Christmas Day.
They dance and sing.
They give **happy** shouts.
They are very glad.
They are as **happy**
as **happy** can be.

hard

A stone is **hard**. It is not soft.
A pillow is soft. It is not **hard**.

Some of the lessons at school are **hard**. They are not easy to do.

has

Jack **has** a boat. He owns the boat. It is his boat. He **has** it in his hand. He holds it in his hand. He **has** to put the boat away. He must put the boat away. He **has** had fun with it.

---

hat

Where do you wear your **hat**?
I wear my **hat** on my head.

---

hate

Jack does not **hate** Jill.
He is fond of Jill.

Pussy hates being out in the rain. She does not like to get wet.

---

hay

Uncle Jack cuts the long grass on his farm. He lets it dry in the sun. Then it is **hay**.

Jack and Jill play in the **hay**.

---

head

Jill has hair on her **head**.
She wears her hat on her **head**.
When her **head** aches, she has a **head**ache.

Jack is **head** of his class.
He is at the top of the class.

See the horse's **head** over the wall.

hear

We **hear** with our ears.
Listen to the music.
Can you **hear** the band playing?
Yes, I can **hear** it.
I have heard it for a long time.
Granny cannot **hear** well. She is deaf.

heart

Your **heart** is in your body. It sends blood through your body. The **heart** is the engine which keeps your body going. You can feel your **heart** beat.
It is pumping blood when it beats.

heat

The sun is very warm.
Can you feel the **heat**?
The sun heats the earth.
The fire heats the room.
It makes the room hot.

heavy

A balloon is light. It is not **heavy**.
Jill can blow a balloon.

A table is **heavy**. It is not light.
Jill cannot blow a table.

help

Jill is learning to sew. Mother will show her how to sew.
She will **help** Jill. Jill helped Mother to wash the dishes.
Jack is helping Dad in the garden.

hen

Nine, ten,
A good fat **hen**.

A **hen** sits on a nest. It lays eggs.
Young hens are called chickens.

A **hen** has two legs.
A **hen** has feathers on its body.

hide

Jack and Jill play **hide**-and-seek.
Jack hides from Jill.
Can you see where he is hiding?
He has hidden up the tree.
Last time he hid behind a bush.

high

Jill is on the ground. Jack is **high** up in the tree.
Jack is higher than Jill. The sky is highest of all.

hill

A **hill** is high.
A mountain is higher.
A mountain is a big **hill**.

Jack and Jill climb up the **hill**.

hold

Jill is on a swing. She can **hold**
on to the rope with one hand. She
can **hold** an apple in the other
hand. She is holding the rope.
She has held the apple.

hole

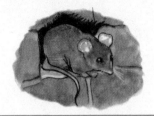

Jack has a **hole** in his sock.
The mouse lives in a **hole** in the wall.
Dad digs a **hole** in the ground.

---

home

Where is Jill?
She is at **home**.

She is in the house where she lives with her family.

---

hope

I **hope** it will be a sunny day.
I wish it would be sunny.
Jill hopes so, too. We are all hoping.

---

horse

A **horse** is an animal. A pony is a small **horse**. How
many legs has a **horse**? A **horse** and cow have the same
number of legs.

There are many kinds of horses. A baby **horse** is a foal.

---

hot

Take off your coat if you are too **hot**.
The sun is **hot**.
The fire is **hot**.
The tea is too **hot** to drink.
Wait till it cools. Then it will not be **hot**.

hour

A sunshiny shower
Won't last half an **hour**.

An **hour** is part of a day. There are twenty-four in a day.

---

house

A **house** is a home where people live.
Jill has a doll's **house**. Milly and Molly live in it.

---

how

" **How** do you do ? And **how** are you ? "
" I'm very well, I thank you."
" **How** can you fib ? It isn't true ;
I saw your mother spank you."

Mother shows Jill **how** to sew. She shows Jill the way to sew. She is teaching Jill **how** to sew.

---

hungry

Jack is **hungry** when he gets up. He wants to eat some food. He is ready for breakfast.

Spot is always **hungry**.

---

hurt

Jack was in such a hurry that he did not see the big stone. He fell over it. He has **hurt** his knee. His knee is sore. It is hurting.

I i *i*

I

I am a girl. I am six. I have a brother called Jack.
Who am **I** ? **I** am Jill.

---

ice

I am as cold as **ice**.
Ice is frozen water.
There is **ice** on the pond.
There are icicles on the walls.
Jack and Jill like to eat **ice**-cream.

---

if

If all the world was paper,
And all the sea was ink ;
If all the trees were bread and cheese,
What should we have to drink ?

If it is a good day, we are going to the sea.
We must stay at home, **if** it rains.

---

ill

Jack is in bed. He is feeling **ill**. He is sick.
Jack is **ill**. He has an illness. He will soon be well.

I'll

I'll means I will. **I'll** go means I will go.

in

Where is Spot? He is **in** the kennel. He went inside. He has gone into the kennel.
Pussy is not **in** the kennel. She is outside.

---

inch

An **inch** is 2½ times as long as a centimetre.

One foot is the same as twelve inches or thirty centimetres.

---

ink

Dad writes with a pen and **ink**. The **ink** is in a bottle. Dad fills his pen with **ink**.

---

insect

The bee is an **insect**. Insects fly about in the air.
An **insect** has six legs.

---

island

There is an **island** in the lake. There is water all round the **island**.
Ireland is an **island**. There is water all round Ireland.

---

it

Jack has a ball. **It** is a cricket ball. Its colour is brown.

J j *j*

jacket

Dad wears an old **jacket** when he works in the garden.
A **jacket** is a short coat.

jail

A bad man tried to steal Jack's bicycle.
The policeman caught the bad man.
He took the bad man to **jail**. The bad
man will be locked up in the **jail**.
A **jail** is a prison.

jam

Jam is made from fruit.
We eat **jam**. We spread **jam** on bread.
What kind of **jam** do you like best?
Do you like strawberry **jam** or plum **jam** or gooseberry
jam? Clear jam is called jelly.

January

January brings the snow,
Makes our feet and fingers glow.

January is a month. There are twelve months in a year.
There are 12.

January   February   March   April   May   June
July August September October November December

jar

We put jam in a **jar**. It is a glass **jar**. A **jar** of jam.

The Forty Thieves hid in big jars.

Jesus

Jesus is the Son of God.

---

join

The children **join** hands. They are going to dance in a ring. They put their hands together. Pussy wants to **join** in. She wants to take part in the fun.

---

jolly

" Ha-ha-ha ! " laughed the **jolly** old man,
And " Ha-ha-ha ! " laughed he.
" I'm **jolly** all night and **jolly** all day,
As **jolly** as **jolly** can be."

The **jolly** man is full of fun. He is very merry. Uncle Jack is a **jolly** man.

---

jug

There is a handle on the **jug**.
The **jug** is full of milk.
It is a milk **jug**.

July

July is a month. There are twelve months in a year. There are 12.

January   February   March   April   May   June
July August September October November December

---

jump

Jack's pony can **jump** over the fence. The pony leaps into the air. Then it goes over the fence, and lands on its feet. It is jumping.

June

June brings tulips, lilies, roses,
Fills the children's hands with posies.

June is a month. There are twelve months in a year. There are 12.

January   February   March   April   May   **June**
July August September October November December

---

jungle

Wild animals live in the **jungle**. There are thick bushes and trees in the **jungle**.

K k *k*

---

kangaroo A **kangaroo** is a wild animal. Its home is in Australia. You can see a **kangaroo** in the zoo. Mother **Kangaroo** carries her baby in her pouch.

---

keep Jack gave Jill a book for her birthday. Jill will **keep** the book. She will take care of it, and have it for a long time. She will **keep** the book in the bookcase. She has kept her dolls for a long time. Jack keeps his knife in his pocket.

---

kettle

K is for **kettle**, so useful to me,
For boiling the water, and making the tea.

We put water in the **kettle**. Then we heat the **kettle** to make the water hot.

---

key Dad locks the door at night. He locks it with a **key**.
There are different kinds of **keys** on the piano.
When you hit the **keys**, you play the piano.

kick

Jack can **kick** his football. He kicks it with his foot. He hits the football with his foot. He is kicking.

The cow kicked the pail.

kind

Mother is **kind** to Jack and Jill. She is good to them. She takes care of them. She is a **kind** mother.
What **kind** of game shall we play? Choose what **kind** of sweet you like best.

king

The **King** of Hearts called for the tarts.

The **King** is a great man. He is the head of all the people in his country. He wears a crown on his head. His wife is called a Queen.

kitchen

Cinderella worked in the **kitchen**. She washed and scrubbed and cooked in the **kitchen**.

kite

Jack is flying his **kite**. Dad made the **kite**. It is made of light wood and paper. The wind carries the **kite** through the air.

kitten

Three little kittens they lost their mittens,
And they began to cry.

A **kitten** is a young cat.

knee

Jill is kneeling on one **knee**.
She is playing with the kitten.
Jill has two knees. She can bend
her knees. **Her knee** is part of
her leg.

knife

We use a **knife** and fork at dinner.
We cut food with the **knife**. The **knife** is sharp.
Jack keeps a **knife** in his pocket. It is a pocket-**knife**.

knock

Knock at the door.
Take care not to **knock** the cup off the table.
Knock the ball to Jack. Hit the ball.

know

Do you **know** who this is ? Yes, I **know**. I am sure it is
Santa Claus. Everybody knows Santa Claus. I knew it was
Santa Claus when I saw his picture.

L 1 *l*

ladder

Jack climbs up the **ladder**.
He wants to reach the apples
at the top of the tree.

lake

An island is land with water all round it.
A **lake** is water with land all round it.

The boys and girls sail their boats on the **lake**.
The swans swim in the **lake**.

lamb

The lambs frisk and play.
They are feeling happy.
A **lamb** is a young sheep.

lame

The horse is **lame**. It has a sore foot. It cannot walk.

land

The ship is on the sea.
The lambs are on **land**.
The **land** is the ground.

Jack jumps down from the tree. He lands on his feet.
He lives in a **land** called Britain.
Uncle Tom lives in a **land** called Canada.

lap

Pussy likes to sit in Jill's **lap**.
Pussy laps up milk with her tongue.
She is lapping milk. She is drinking it.

large

A doll's house is small.

Jill's home is **large**. It is larger than the doll's home.

A castle is the largest of the three.

last

Jack and Jill ran a race. Jack was first. Jill was **last**.
How long will the rain **last**? It will not **last** long. It will soon be over.
Last night I saw the moon.
December is the **last** month in the year.

late

Jack is **late** in getting up. He went to bed **late** last night.
He will be **late** for school. Jill will be later. She is still in bed. She will get up later. She will get up after a while.

laugh

The clown stood on his head at the circus. He made the children **laugh**.
" Ha-ha-ha ! " laughed Jack.
" Ha-ha-ha ! " laughed Jill.
They were laughing at the funny clown.
You could hear their laughter.

lead

Jill has to **lead** her pony out of the stable. She guides her pony.
She goes first to **lead** the way. She is leading the pony. She has led the way.

leaf

In Spring the leaves on the trees are green. The trees are leafy.
In Autumn the leaves fall off the trees.
A **leaf** grows on a tree or plant.

leap

Jack is going to **leap** over the fence.
He is going to jump over.
He will be leaping.
He will be jumping.

learn

Jill goes to school to **learn** how to read and write.
She will find out how to read and write.

leave   You must **leave** home in time to go to school. Go away from home.
Leave Pussy at home. She cannot go to school.
Are you leaving Pussy? Yes, I have left her.

left   Your **left** hand is on your **left** arm.
Your right hand is on the other arm.
Jill has an apple in her **left** hand.

leg   Jill has one left **leg** and one right **leg**. She has two legs.
A cow has four legs. An insect has six legs.

lemon   A **lemon** is a fruit. It grows on a tree. The juice of lemons is sour. We put sugar in it to make it sweet.

A **lemon** is yellow when it is ripe.
We make lemonade from lemons.

letter   The postman has brought a **letter** for Jill. She reads the **letter**. The **letter** is from Aunt Jane. It was in an envelope.
Aunt Jane puts her address at the top of the **letter**.
The **letter** begins, " Dear Jill ".
Can you write a **letter** ?

lid

Here is a box. It has a **lid**.
The **lid** is not on the box.
Put the **lid** on the box.

There are lids on our eyes. They are eyelids. You cannot see when your eyelids are closed.

---

lie

Never tell a **lie**. Never say a thing that is not true.
When you tell a **lie**, you are lying.
When you have told a **lie**, you have lied.
The cat lay on the rug. It likes lying by the fire.
We **lie** in bed at night.

---

life

Everything that is alive has **life**.
Animals have **life**. Trees and plants have **life**.
A table is not alive. It does not grow. It has no **life**.
Jack is full of **life**. He is very lively.

---

lift

Jill can **lift** the jug. She can take it up in her hand.
Jill cannot **lift** the table. It is too heavy to **lift**.

---

like

The two rabbits look the same.
They look **like** each other.
They are alike. Rabbits **like** to eat lettuce. They enjoy eating it.

line

Can you draw a straight **line**? Here is a line. ——————
The boys and girls are standing in a **line**.
Hang the clothes on the clothes-**line**.

lion

Look at the **lion**. He is a wild
animal. He is called the king of
animals, because he is so strong.
As strong as a **lion**.
You can see a **lion** in the zoo.

listen

Listen to Mother. She is telling us a story.
We **listen** with our ears.

little

Little Poll Parrot
Sat in his garret,
Eating toast and tea;
A **little** brown mouse
Jumped into the house,
And stole it all away.

The calf is **little**. The cow is big.

live

We cannot **live** without food. We would die without food.
Dad waters the flowers in the garden to keep them alive.
They will **live** and grow.
Where does Jack **live**? He lives in a house. He has lived
there for seven years.
Foxes **live** in dens. Birds **live** in nests.

load

The donkey has a **load** on its back. The donkey has a heavy weight to carry. The man is loading the donkey. He is putting a **load** on the donkey's back.

loaf

Mother cuts slices of bread from a **loaf**. The baker bakes loaves of bread.

long

This is a short dog.

This is a **long** dog. Its body is longer than the other dog's body.

Uncle Tom has been abroad for a **long** time. He has been away for many years. Jill longs to see him again. She is longing for him to come back. She wants him to come back.

look

Look at this picture. Are you looking at it? What can you see? What does it **look** like? You can see Pussy looking at herself in the looking-glass. She can see herself when she looks in the glass.

Jill has been looking for Pussy. She cannot find Pussy.

loose   The horse has been let **loose**. He runs round the field.
He has shoe is **loose**. It will come off.

lose   The horse will **lose** his shoe. No one will be able to find it.
Jill lost Pussy. She looked for her, and found her.

lot   Jack has a **lot** of marbles.
He has many marbles.
Tom has only a few marbles.
He has not a **lot**.

loud   The lion gives a **loud** roar. You can hear it a long way off.
It is so noisy.
A whisper is not **loud**.
A roar is **loud**.

low    There is a squirrel at the top of
the tree. He is high up. There is
a squirrel near the foot of the tree.
He is **low** down. He is lower
down than the other squirrel.

lump   This is a **lump** of coal.   This is a **lump** of sugar.
It is a piece of coal.   It is a piece of sugar.

M m *m*

machine   Most things we use are made by machines. This book was made by machines. There are many different kinds of machines.

Dad's car is a **machine**.

Jack's bicycle is a **machine**.

An aeroplane is a flying-**machine**.

The farmer uses machines to help him with his work.

Mother has a sewing-**machine**.

magic

Jill reads about **magic** in her fairy stories. The Fairy Queen waved her wand. She changed the frog into a prince. It was **magic**.

make

Dad can **make** a bird-house. He can build a little house for the birds. When it is made, the birds will come and visit it. They will **make** a noise. They will sing. Dad likes making things. He makes Jack help him.

man

Dad is a **man**. Mother is a woman.
Jack will grow up to be a **man**.
Jill will grow up to be a woman.

many

How **many** days are in a week?
There are seven days in a week.
There are **many** days in a year.
There are a great number of days in a year.

map

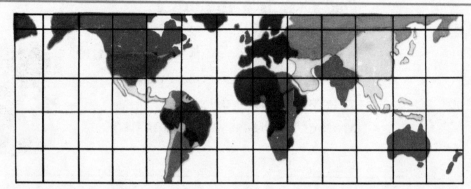

This is a **map** of the world. Look at the **map,** and see if
you can find the country where you live.

marble

Jack and Tom like to play a game with marbles.
A **marble** is round and hard. It is often made of glass.

March

March winds and April showers
Bring forth the sweet May flowers.

March is a month. There are twelve months in a year.
There are 12.

January   February   **March**   April   May   June
July   August   September   October   November   December

march

Jack is marching with the soldiers.
They are out for a **march**.
They are moving in order.
They are keeping in step with each other. Left, right! Left!

---

market

To **market**, to **market**, to buy a fat pig,
Home again, home again, jiggety jig.

A **market** is a place where things are bought and sold.

---

match

The two penguins **match**.
They are alike.

The crow and the penguin do not **match**. They are not alike.

Dad is at a football-**match**.
He lights his pipe with a **match**.

---

matter

Oh dear! what can the **matter** be?

What is wrong? It is only a little **matter** that is wrong.
Pussy has spilt her milk, but it does not **matter** much.

May

May is a month. **May** day is the first day in **May**. The **May** Queen is crowned Queen of the **May**.

There are twelve months in a year. There are 12.

January February March April **May** June July August September October November December

---

me

Jack and Jill found a frog.
" Give it to **me**," said Jack.
" It is mine."
" Give it to **me**," said Jill.
" It is mine."
" It belongs to **me**," said Jack.
" It belongs to **me**," said Jill.
But the frog said, " You can't catch **me**," and away it hopped.

---

meal

What **meal** do you eat in the morning ?
We have breakfast in the morning.
When we eat food, we have a **meal**.
Little Miss Muffet was eating curds
and whey. She was having a **meal**.

---

mean

Jill fell into the pond. She did not **mean** to do it. It was an accident.
Does she **mean** to tell Mother ? Has she made up her mind to tell Mother ? Yes, she means to tell Mother. It would be **mean** of her not to tell. It would not be right.

measure

Jack will weigh himself on the machine, to find out how heavy he is. The weighing-machine measures weight. It will show how many kilograms Jack weighs.

Dad will **measure** Jack to find out how tall he is. He will **measure** him with a long ruler. It will show how many metres and centimetres Jack is in height. A clock measures time. Mother has a tape **measure**.

meet

The kitten is running down the road. Pussy is running towards her. They will **meet**.
The kitten has gone to **meet** Pussy. She wants to be beside Pussy. She likes meeting Pussy.

merry

Old King Cole was a **merry** old soul.

He was always happy and laughing.
We are happy on Christmas Day. We say, "A **Merry** Christmas."

merry-go-round

Jack and Jill rode on the **merry-go-round** at the fair.

middle

There was a little girl
And she had a little curl
Right in the **middle** of her forehead ;
And when she was good
She was very, very good,
But when she was bad she was horrid.

The **middle** is the centre. When we halve anything, we cut it through the **middle**.

midnight

Midnight is twelve o'clock at night. The day comes to an end at **midnight**.

milk

We get **milk** from cows. We drink **milk**. The milkman brings our **milk** in bottles. The milkmaid is milking the cow.

mind

Jill remembers the stories she reads. She keeps them in her **mind**. She thinks with her **mind**.
She does not **mind** if Jack reads her books. She does not care. She lets Jack read them. She tells him to **mind** them. She tells him to take care of them.

mine

Jill has a teddy-bear. Jill says, " It is my teddy. Teddy is **mine**. He belongs to me."
There are mines in the earth. They are deep holes. We get coal and metal from mines.

minute

Tick-tock! says the clock. It is ticking away the seconds and the minutes and the hours.
There are sixty seconds in a **minute**. There are 60.
There are sixty minutes in an hour. There are 60.
There are twenty-four hours in a day. There are 24.

Can you tell what time it is on the clock?
It is ten minutes past nine.
It is 10 minutes past 9.

miss

Mother has gone to visit Uncle Jack. The children **miss** her. They wish she would come back.

Jack has hit his thumb with the hammer. He tried to hit the nail, but he missed it. Dad said, "You should aim at the nail. Then you will not **miss** it."

Jill has to run for the bus, or she will **miss** it. She will have to hurry to catch it. Pussy has run away. She is missing.

mix

Jack can **mix** the colours in his paint-box. He mixes blue and yellow to make green.

Mother can **mix** flour and sugar and butter and eggs together in a bowl. When she has mixed them she puts them in a tin. She puts the tin in the oven and bakes a cake.

Monday

Solomon Grundy,
 Born on a **Monday**,
  Christened on Tuesday,
   Married on Wednesday,
    Took ill on Thursday,
     Worse on Friday,
      Died on Saturday,
       Buried on Sunday.
        That is the end of Solomon Grundy.

Monday is one of the days of the week.
There are seven days in a week. There are 7.

money

Dad earns **money**. He earns pounds and pence. We pay for things with **money**.
Dad saves some **money**. The bank looks after the **money** for him. Mother keeps **money** in a purse.

monkey

A **monkey** is an animal. The **monkey** at the circus did funny tricks. He swung on a rope. He stood on his head. He gave Jill a nut.

month

A year is divided into twelve months. A **month** is part of a year. Can you say the names of the months? In which **month** were you born?

moon
The Man in the **Moon**
Came tumbling down.

Can you see a man in the **moon**?
The **moon** shines at night.
It gives **moon**light.

---

more
Would you like **more** tea? Do you want another cup of tea?
Jack has a lot of marbles. He has **more** marbles than Tom.
Jack has most of the marbles. He has nearly all the marbles.

---

morning
Good-**morning**. It is time to get up. The **morning** is the first part of the day. The cock crows early in the **morning**.

---

mother
Mother is Dad's wife. She is Jack and Jill's **mother**. They are her children.
Pussy is the kitten's **mother**.
The cow is the calf's **mother**.

---

mouse
A **mouse** is an animal. It has four legs.
It has a long tail. It has whiskers.
How many mice can you see in the picture?

---

mouth
Dad puts his pipe in his **mouth**.
Jill puts a sweet in her **mouth**.
We eat and speak with our mouths.

move

The men are going to **move** the piano.
They are going to put it in a different
place. They are moving the piano.
Jack can **move** quickly when he runs.

---

music

Merry are the bells, and merry would they ring,
Merry was myself, and merry could I sing;
With a merry ding-dong, happy, gay, and free,
And a merry sing-song, happy let us be.

When the bells ring, they make **music**.
When we sing, we make **music**.
When we play the piano, we make **music**.
A band plays **music**.
The cat is playing the fiddle. He is
making **music**.

---

my

"This is **my** snowman," says Jack. "I made him myself.
He is mine. He is **my** snowman." "Oh, **my**!" says the
snowman. "Wait till the sun shines. Then I will melt. **My**
arms will melt. **My** nose will melt. **My** head will melt.
My body will melt away." "**My, my**!" says the Sun.
"Here I come with **my** bright rays. **My** heat will melt
you."

N n *n*

nail

Jill has a **nail** on each finger. She has ten fingernails. Jill has a **nail** on each toe. She has ten toenails.

A bird's claw is its **nail**.

Dad hits a **nail** with his hammer. He is nailing two pieces of wood together.

name

Everybody has a **name**. Jill's **name** is Jill Brown. Jack's **name** is Jack Brown. The dog's **name** is Spot. The dog is named Spot.
What is your **name**? Can you spell your **name**?
Daisy is the **name** of a flower.

navy

Jack wants to be a sailor. He will join the **navy** when he grows up. He will sail on a ship. There are many ships in the **navy**.

near

America is far away from Britain. It is not **near**. Canada is nearer to America than Britain. When you are in Canada, you are nearly in America. You are almost there.

neck

Jack wears his tie round his **neck**.
Jack's head is above his **neck**. His
shoulders are below his **neck**.
Punch and Judy's dog, Toby, has a
frill round its **neck**.

---

need

We **need** food to keep us alive.
We must have food to live.

---

needle

This is a **needle** and thread. We sew
with a **needle**. A **needle** has a sharp
point. It has a hole at the other end. The
hole is the **needle's** eye. We put the
thread through the eye.

---

neither

Is this a cow or a dog?
It is **neither** a cow nor a dog.
It is not a cow. It is not a dog.
It is a crocodile.

---

nest

What does little birdie say
In her **nest** at peep of day?

A **nest** is a bird's home. The birds build nests in trees and
bushes. They lay eggs in their nests.

---

never

Jack has **never** seen a giant.
He has not ever seen a giant.
Jill has **never** seen a fairy.

new

Jack has a **new** pair of shoes. He has just bought them. He has not worn them yet. They are **new** shoes.

The chicken is newly born. It is just coming out of the shell. It is a **new** chicken.

Every morning a **new** day begins.

---

next

Jack is drawing a picture. What is he going to do **next**?
What will he do after he has drawn the picture?
He will paint the picture **next**.
His brush is beside the paint-box. It is next to the paint-box.

---

night

Good-**night**! It is time to go to bed.
The early part of the day is the morning.
The late part of the day is the **night**. It is dark at **night**.

---

nine

Nine is a number. It is **9**.
Can you see **nine** stars in the sky?

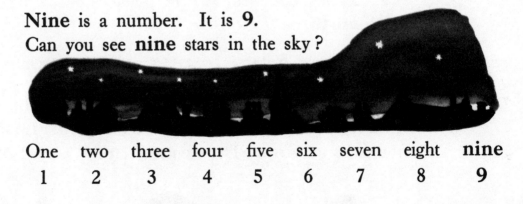

One	two	three	four	five	six	seven	eight	**nine**
1	2	3	4	5	6	7	8	**9**

---

nobody

Dad, Mother, Jack and Jill have gone out.
There is no person in the house. There is **nobody** at home.

nod

Spot is a clever dog. He can do tricks. He can **nod** his head when he wants to say, "Yes." He makes his head go up and down. He is nodding.

none

There were two birds sitting on a stone,
One flew away and then there was one.
The other flew after and then there was **none**,
And so the poor stone was left all alone.

north

There are four points of the earth. They are **north**, south, east, west. Hold a stick upright in your hand at noon. The shadow will point to the **north**.

North

West   East

South

nose

Jill's **nose** is in the middle of her face. She can breathe through her **nose**. She can smell with her **nose**. A bird's beak is its **nose**. The elephant's trunk is its **nose**.

not Jill is **not** going to school today. She is **not** well.

---

nothing Jack's pockets are empty.
There is not a thing in them.
There is **nothing** in his pockets.

November Dull **November** brings the blast,
Then the leaves are whirling fast.

November is the name of a month. There are twelve months in a year. There are 12.

January	February	March	April	May	June	July
1	2	3	4	5	6	7

August	September	October	November	December
8	9	10	11	12

---

now It is raining **now**. It is raining at this time.

---

number A **number** is a measure which tells you how many things there are. Jack has one bicycle. Jill has two eyes. The cat has four paws. One, two, and four are numbers.

Can you fill in the numbers?

........Blind Mice.   ....Dwarfs.   ....Ugly Sisters.

O O *O*

---

oak
An **oak** is a tree. It grows from an acorn into a big tree. The **oak** lives for hundreds of years.

---

obey

Jack's dog will **obey** him. " Come here, Spot," calls Jack. Spot does what he is told. He comes to Jack. He obeys Jack. He is obeying Jack's orders.

---

o'clock
What time is noon ?
It is noon at twelve **o'clock** midday.
It is noon at twelve by the clock.

October
October is the name of a month. There are twelve months in a year. There are 12.

January February March April May June July

August September **October** November December

of

Jill is reading the story **of** Cinderella. She reads about Cinderella. She knows most **of** the story already. Cinderella's dress was made **of** rags. She worked in the kitchen **of** her Ugly Sisters. The kitchen belonged to her Ugly Sisters. They were the sisters **of** Cinderella.

off

The Ugly Sisters have gone **off** to the ball. They have gone away to the ball. Cinderella takes her apron **off**. She unties her apron, and puts it away.

often

Jill has never seen a giant. She has **often** seen a clown. She has seen a clown many times.

oh

Jack found a hedgehog in the garden. " **Oh** ! What a surprise," cried Jack. Jack did not expect to see the hedge-hog. He was very surprised.

old

Old Mother Goose when
She wanted to wander,
Would ride through the air
On a very fine gander.

Mother Goose was not young. She was **old**.
Jack is seven years of age. He is not **old**. He is young.
Jill is six years **old**. Jack is older than Jill.
Granny is the oldest in the family.
Dad wears **old** clothes when he works in the garden.

---

on

Pussy is sitting **on** the rug. Jill is sitting **on** a chair.
She is putting her shoes **on**.
On Monday she bought new shoes. She will have them **on**
today for the first time. She had been for a ride **on** her pony.

---

one

There is **one** duck on the water.
There is **one** duck on the land.
One and **one** make two.
One is a number. It is number
one. It is **1**.

---

only

There is **only** one duck on the pond. It is the **only** one.
There is just one duck on the pond.

---

open

The first door is **open**.

The second door is shut.

orange

An **orange** is a fruit. It grows on an **orange** tree. Peel the skin off before you eat the **orange**. The skin is **orange** in colour.

This is the colour of **orange**.

---

order

Everything on the table is out of **order**. Can you see what is wrong? Could you put the table in **order**?

Spot obeys Jack's **order**. "Bring the ball," orders Jack. Spot brings the ball. He does what Jack has ordered. Jack keeps Spot in good **order**. He brushes and looks after Spot, in **order** to keep him well.

Mother goes to the shop to **order** things. She tells the shop-keeper what she wants.

---

other

Would you like an apple or an orange? You may have one or the **other**. You may have an apple or an orange.
Jill likes sums, but the **other** children do not like them. The rest of the children do not like sums.
Jill has no **other** brother but Jack. She has no more brothers.

---

our

Jack and Jill have a little garden of their own. "It is **our** garden," say Jack and Jill. "It belongs to us. It is ours. We work in it ourselves."

over

The old witch is flying **over** the houses. She is flying above the houses. She has an umbrella **over** her head. It is above her head. She is going to fly **over** the sea. She will fly across the sea. If it is windy, she might fall **over**.

She has flown **over** and **over** again. She has flown many times. She has flown **over** a hundred times. When the day is **over**, she will be away **over** the sea.

owl

There was an old Man with a beard,
Who said, " It is just as I feared !
Two Owls and a Hen,
Four Larks and a Wren,
Have all built their nests in my beard."

The **owl** is a bird. What other birds are in the poem ? The **owl** sleeps through the day. It flies about at night.

ox

An **ox** is an animal. It belongs to the cow family. Oxen is the name for more than one **ox**. In some countries oxen draw ploughs and carts.

P p *p*

pack

Pack your toys into the cupboard. Put them in the cupboard. **Pack** your clothes in a suitcase. Are you packing them? The old man carries a **pack** on his back. He has a bundle on his back.

paddle

Jack and Jill like to **paddle** at the seaside. They skip about on their bare feet at the edge of the water.

Dad takes them out in a canoe. It is a kind of boat. Its oar is called a **paddle**. Dad can **paddle** the canoe.

page

There are many pages in Jill's story-book. She reads one **page**. Then she turns over a **page** and reads the next **page**. How many pages are in this book?

pain

Jill has been stung by a bee. She is hurt. She feels **pain**. Her arm is sore. She has a **pain** in her arm. Her arm is painful.

pair A **pair** is two of a kind.

A **pair** of socks.   A **pair** of shoes.   A **pair** of gloves.

---

palm

This is a **palm** tree.   This is the **palm** of the hand.

---

panda

A **panda** is a large animal. It is a wild animal, but can easily be tamed. It chirps like a bird, and squeals when it is afraid.

---

pansy A **pansy** is a flower. Some pansies grow wild, and some grow in gardens. There are pansies of many colours. The flowers look as if they were made of velvet.

---

paper This book is made of **paper**. There is **paper** on the wall. It is wall**paper**. We wrap up parcels with **paper**. The news**paper** is made of **paper**.

---

park Jack and Jill go to the **park** to play. There is grass in the **park**, and trees and flowers. There is a pond in the **park**.

part

This is a whole cake.

This is **part** of a cake.
It is a piece of the cake.

Jack and Jill **part** from each other in the morning. They leave each other, and go off to different schools. Jill will play the **part** of Cinderella at the party. She will **part** her hair in the middle.

party

Jill's friends came to her birthday **party**. They played games. They wore paper hats. They had good things to eat. It was a lovely **party**.

pass

The car is going to **pass** the horse and cart. It will go on in front of them.

The rain will soon **pass**. It will soon be over.
Please **pass** the salt. Please hand the salt to me.
Will you **pass** your test at school? If I work hard, I shall get through my test.

past

The car is passing the horse and cart. Soon it will be **past**. It will have gone by the horse and cart.
What time is it? It is half **past** one.
It is half an hour after one o'clock.

path   A long winding **path** led to the little house in the wood. The **path** was a narrow road where people could walk to the house. There is a **path** in Dad's garden.

paw   Jill walks on her feet. Pussy walks on her paws. Pussy has a **paw** on each foot. She has four paws. The foot of an animal with claws is called a **paw**.

pay   There is a ball in the shop window. Jack wants to buy the ball. He has to **pay** the shopkeeper for the ball. He gives the shopkeeper money. He has paid for the ball. The ball is his.

Dad gets paid for his work. He gives some of his **pay** to Mother. She buys food with the money.

pea   A **pea** is a vegetable. Peas grow in pods in the garden. We take the peas out of the pods and cook them. We eat the peas.

A sweet **pea** is a flower. It grows in many different colours.

peach   A **peach** is a fruit. It grows on a **peach** tree. Peaches are very good to eat.

peacock   A **peacock** is a bird. It has a lovely tail, with many colours in it. The **peacock** spreads its tail out like a fan. It is a proud bird. We say a proud person is as proud as a **peacock**.

---

pear

A **pear** is a fruit. It grows on a **pear** tree. Pears are very good to eat.

This is a **pear**.   This is a peach.

---

peel   Take the skin off before you eat the peach. **Peel** the skin off.

---

pen   Dad writes with a **pen**. He fills his **pen** with ink.

---

pencil   Jack writes with a **pencil**. He has a red **pencil** and a blue **pencil**. He keeps his pencils in a **pencil** case.

---

penguin   Look at the penguins! There is one **penguin** in the water, and one **penguin** on land. A **penguin** can swim. A **penguin** can walk about on the land.

penny
A **penny** is a coin. It is money.
There are one hundred pence in a pound. There are **100**.

---

people
When they saw the Queen, all the **people** cheered.
Every person cheered when they saw the Queen.

---

pet
I had a little Doggy that used to sit and beg,
But Doggy tumbled down the stairs and broke his little leg.
Oh! Doggy, I will nurse you, and try to make you well,
And you shall have a collar with a little silver bell.

The dog is the little girl's **pet**.
She looks after him and pets him.
The lamb was Mary's **pet**. It
was a **pet** lamb.
Spot is Jack's **pet**.
Pussy is Jill's **pet**.
Jill pets Pussy.

---

piano
Jill is learning to play the **piano**.
She is making music on the **piano**.
She sits at the **piano**. She strikes
the **piano** keys with her fingers.
She can play tunes on the **piano**.

---

pick
Spot can **pick** up a ball in his mouth. He lifts the ball up
with his mouth. Jill likes to **pick** apples from the tree. She
pulls the apples off the tree. She picks out the one she wants
to eat. She chooses which one she will eat.

picnic

The teddy-bears are having a **picnic**. They are having a meal out of doors.
Jack and Jill like to have a **picnic**, too.

picture

Can you see a **picture** on this page? There are many pictures in this book. Pictures show you what things are like, and what people are doing. Jack likes to draw pictures. Mother hangs pictures on the wall.

pig

Tom, Tom, the piper's son,
Stole a **pig**, and away he run!

A **pig** is an animal. The farmer keeps pigs in the pigsty. They make a noise like " Grumph-grumph ! "

pigeon

A **pigeon** is a bird. It belongs to the dove family. Some pigeons are very tame. Some pigeons can carry messages. They are carrier pigeons.

pin

See a **pin** and pick it up,
All the day you'll have good luck.

A **pin** is used to fasten things together. It pins things together. A **pin** is sharp at one end. Pins are straight. Safety-pins fasten with a little catch. They are not straight.

pink

Pink is a colour. It is pale red. Jill's cheeks are **pink**. She has a **pink** ribbon on her hair.

This is **pink**.

pipe

Dad smokes a **pipe**. He fills the **pipe** with tobacco. He puts the **pipe** in his mouth. He lights the tobacco. Then he puffs at his **pipe**. He is smoking his **pipe**.
A different kind of **pipe** carries water or gas. It is a kind of long tube.

place

Jack and Jill take their places at the table. Jack's **place** is beside Mother. Jill's **place** is beside Dad. Dad's **place** is at the head of the table. Mother will **place** the food on the table. She will put the food on the table.

plan

Dad has had a fine **plan**. He has had a good idea. He has planned to take the children for a trip. He has thought out the trip. He drew a **plan** to show which places the children would visit.

plate   Jill has a blue **plate** for her soup.

She has a pink **plate** for her pudding.

Mother keeps the plates in the cupboard. She uses the plates at meal times. She puts food on the plates.

---

play   Boys and girls come out to **play**. What game shall we **play**? Let us **play** with balloons.
Jill can **play** the piano. She can make music on the piano.
Punch and Judy act in a **play**. They **play** a part.
Dad likes playing golf. He is a good player.

---

playground   A **playground** is a place at school or in the park. Children play in the **playground**.

---

please   Good little boys should never say
" I will," and " Give me these."
Oh, no! that never is the way,
But " Mother, if you **please**!"

It will **please** Mother if you are polite.
Say " **please** " when you ask for something.

plenty

The king was in his counting-house
Counting out his money.

The king had **plenty** of money.
He had enough money for everything he wanted to buy.

plough

To **plough**, and sow, and reap, and mow,
And be a farmer's boy.

The farmer's boy is ploughing.
The **plough** turns over the soil,
ready for sowing the seeds.

poem

A **poem** is a piece of poetry. It is a kind of story in verse.
A man who writes poems is called a poet.
Here is a **poem**:

Minnie and Winnie slept in a shell.
Sleep, little ladies! And they slept well.

policeman

What is the **policeman** doing?
He is holding up his hand to stop
the motor cars. He will let the
old woman cross the street in safety.
Policemen take care of us. They
see that everybody keeps the law.
They take bad men to prison.

pony

Yankee Doodle came to town
Riding on a **pony**;
Stuck a feather in his cap
And called it Macaroni.

Jack and Jill have ponies. They ride their ponies. Jack's **pony**. can jump over a fence.

poor

Poor old Robinson Crusoe!
Poor old Robinson Crusoe!
They made him a coat
Of an old nanny-goat.
I wonder how
They could do so!

We say **poor** Robinson Crusoe, because we are sorry for him. We also say **poor** Robinson Crusoe, because he was a **poor** man. He had no money.

postman

Here is the **postman** bringing the mail. He has two letters for Dad. He has a parcel for Mother. He has a postcard for Jill. He has a magazine for Jack. He has nothing for Pussy.

pot

Mother makes soup in a **pot**.
She uses pots and pans when she is cooking.
She has a plant in a flower**pot**.
She makes tea in the tea**pot**.

pound

A **pound** is a measure of weight.
Mother buys a **pound** of tea and a **pound** of sugar.
A **pound** is also money. It is a hundred pence.

---

pour

Mother is going to **pour** out the tea. The tea will come pouring out of the teapot. It will run out of the teapot.

---

present

Jack is not here at **present**. He is not here at the **present** time. He is not here just now.
He has gone to buy a **present** for Jill. He is buying her a gift. He will **present** it to Jill. He will give it to Jill.

---

pretend

Jack likes to think that he is somebody else. He likes to **pretend**. He is pretending to be an Indian.

---

prince

This is a **prince**. He is the son of a king or a queen.

This is a princess. She is the daughter of a king or a queen.

pudding   We eat **pudding** at dinner. Puddings are sweet. We have plum **pudding** at Christmas.

---

pull   The boys are playing a game. It is tug-of-war. They each **pull** the rope. Each side wants to **pull** the other side over the line. They are all pulling as hard as they can.

---

puma   A **puma** is a wild animal.
It is a kind of wild cat.
The **puma** lives in America.
It is strong enough to kill a horse.

---

pump   Jack has a bicycle **pump**. He pumps air into the tyres with his pump.

---

puppy   The **puppy** is a young dog.
He is trying to chew Dad's slipper.

purple

Purple is a colour.

This is **purple**.

Jill wears a **purple** cloak when she goes to a party.

---

purse

Mother keeps her money in her **purse**.
A **purse** is a little bag.

---

push

Jill is on a swing. She wants Jack to **push** the swing. Jack moves the swing with his hands. He gives the swing a **push**, and away Jill goes. Jack likes pushing the swing.

---

put

Put the teapot on the table. Set the teapot on the table.
Put on your hat. Set your hat on your head.
Jill likes putting a stamp on a letter.
She sticks the stamp on the letter.

Q q *q*

quack

What a noise the ducks are making!
They are saying, " Quack, quack ! "
It is their way of speaking.

quarrel

The ducks are having a **quarrel**. They are angry with each other. They are having a fight.

quarter

There are four boys. There is one apple. Each boy wants a piece of apple. We must divide the apple into four parts.
Cut the apple through the middle. Then it will be in two halves. Cut each half through the middle. Then the apple will be in four quarters.
There will be a **quarter** of an apple for each boy.

queen

A **queen** is the wife of a king.

queer

Twinkle, twinkle, little bat.
How I wonder what you're at !
Up above the world you fly,
Like a tea-tray in the sky !

This is a **queer** poem. It is a strange poem.

---

question

Jill often asks a **question**.
She asks, " What time is it ? "
She asks, " When will Uncle Jack come ? "
She asks, " Will there be honey for tea ? "
Mother tries to answer all Jill's questions.

---

quick

Jack and Jill are having a race on their ponies. Jill's pony is **quick**. It runs very fast. Jack's pony is quicker. It runs faster than Jill's.

---

quiet

Look at the snow falling. It is very **quiet**. It does not make a noise. It comes down quietly.

---

quite

The ground is not **quite** covered with snow. It is almost covered. Soon it will be **quite** covered. It will be all covered.

R r r

rabbit

A **rabbit** is an animal. It lives under the ground in a home called a burrow. Rabbits like to eat the vegetables in the garden. We sometimes call them bunny-rabbits.

race

The hare and the tortoise ran a **race**. The hare was very quick. The tortoise was very slow. The hare was sure that he could **race** the tortoise. He ran half the **race,** then lay down to sleep. He thought he had plenty of time. But he slept too long. The tortoise went on in a slow and steady way. He did not stop. In the end he won the **race**.
Slow and steady wins the **race**.

rag

A **rag** is an old piece of cloth. Cinderella's clothes were old and torn. They were in rags.
The scarecrow is dressed in rags.

railway

The train travels on the **railway**. The rails are laid along the **railway** track. The train runs along the rails.

rain

Oh, where do you come from,
You little drops of **rain**,
Pitter patter, pitter patter,
Down the window pane?

Rain is drops of water. It falls down from the sky on a rainy day.

rat

A **rat** is an animal.
It looks like a big mouse.

reach

Look at the giraffe with his long neck. He can **reach** right up to the top of the tree. He can stretch his neck and eat the leaves at the top. He is reaching for the leaves.

Jack runs fast. He can **reach** home before Jill. He can get home before Jill.

read

Jill can **read** this book. She can look at the book and tell what is written in it. She is reading.

ready

Breakfast is **ready**. Breakfast is on the table. It is time to eat breakfast. Jack is **ready** for breakfast. He is hungry. After breakfast he will be **ready** to go to school.

real

Jill is a **real** girl. Molly is not **real**. She is a doll.

This is a toy duck.

This is a **real** duck.

receive

Jill's pony is fond of sugar. Jill will give sugar to the pony. The pony will **receive** the sugar. It will get the sugar. Jill received the pony from Dad. She got the pony from Dad.

red

Red is a colour.

This is **red**.

Little **Red** Riding Hood wore a **red** cloak and a **red** hood.

rein

Jill uses a **rein** when she is riding her pony. A **rein** is a long strip of leather. Jill uses the **rein** to guide the pony.

reindeer

A **reindeer** is a kind of deer which lives in very cold lands. It can run very fast over the snow. **Reindeer** pull Santa Claus's sledge.

remember

Remember, remember,
The fifth of November.

When Jill reads stories she tries to keep them in mind. She tries to **remember** them. Jack cannot find his hat. He does not **remember** where he put it.

---

reply

"Who killed Cock Robin?"
That is a question.
"I," said the Sparrow,
"With my bow and arrow."

The sparrow has given a **reply** to the question. He has given an answer.

---

rest

Pussy is lying on the rug. She is tired. She is having a **rest**. She will lie there for the **rest** of the day. She will lie there for all the day that is left.

---

ribbon

Jill wears a **ribbon** on her hair.
She ties the **ribbon** round her hair.

---

rice

Rice is the grain of the **rice-**plant. It grows in wet ground, in China, Japan, and India. We cook **rice** and eat it.

---

rich

The king was **rich**. He had plenty of money.
The poor man was not **rich**. He had no money.

riddle

A **riddle** is a puzzle.
Can you guess the answer to this **riddle**?

Higher than a house, higher than a tree.
Oh! whatever can that be?

The answer to this **riddle** is a star.

---

ride

Jack and Jill are having a **ride**
on the camel.
Sometimes they **ride** on their
ponies. They like riding on
their ponies.
Sometimes they **ride** in Dad's car.
Sometimes they **ride** in the train.
They have often ridden in the bus.

---

right

One side of you is the **right** side. The other side is the left.
You write with your **right** hand. That is the **right** way to
write if you are **right**-handed.

---

ring

The elves danced in a **ring**. They danced in a circle.

Jack will **ring** the bell. Mother wears a **ring** on her finger.

river　A **river** is a large stream. It is water that runs to the sea. Ships sail on big rivers. Dad fishes in the **river**.

road

Dad is driving his car along the **road**. He is coming to a bridge across the **road**. The bridge goes over the river.

rob

The Knave of Hearts
He stole the tarts.

The Knave of Hearts wanted to **rob** the Queen. He stole the tarts from the Queen. He was a robber.

robin

Little **Robin** Redbreast sat upon a tree,
Up went Pussy-cat, and down went he.
Down came Pussy-cat, and away **Robin** ran,
Says little **Robin** Redbreast, " Catch me if you can."

A **robin** is a little bird with a red breast. The **robin** sings a sweet song. Jack and Jill feed the robins in winter.

rock　There are some big stones at the seaside. They are called rocks. A **rock** is like a little hill made of stone. There are some big rocks in the sea.
The wind can **rock** the trees. It makes them sway.

roll

Teddy Bear has fallen downstairs. He is going to **roll** down. He will turn over and over.
Jill will **roll** him up in a shawl. She will wrap the shawl round him. She will eat a **roll** for breakfast.

roof

Pussy sometimes sits on the **roof**. She sits on the top of the house. The chimney is on the **roof**. There are slates on the **roof**. They help to keep the rain out.

room

This is Jill's **room**. It is her bed**room**. There is plenty of **room** in it. There is enough space in the **room**.

root

The **root** of a plant is below the ground. The **root** keeps the plant steady, and helps it to grow.
Dad pulls weeds up by the **root**. Then the weeds die.

rope

Jill's swing is made of **rope**. **Rope** is a strong kind of string. We tie up big parcels with **rope**. We **rope** the parcels.

rose

A **rose** is a flower. Some roses grow in the garden. Some roses grow wild. There are many colours of roses. Roses have a sweet perfume.

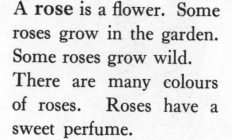

round

The world is **round**. It is shaped like a ball.
Jack and Jill walk **round** the park.
They walk in a circle in the park.
Spot has a collar **round** his neck. The collar is about his neck. Jill wears a belt **round** her waist.

row

The kittens are in a **row**. They are in a straight line.
Dad can **row** a boat. He can make the boat travel through the water.

rub

Jack helps Dad to clean the car. Jack will **rub** the car with a cloth. He will clean the dirt off. He likes rubbing the car.

rubber

Jill has made a mistake in her sum. She rubs out the mistake with a **rubber**. The **rubber** wipes out what she has written. Then she tries to do the sum again.
Rubber comes from a **rubber** tree.

rude

Jack is a polite boy. He is not **rude**.
Rude boys are not polite.

---

rug

There is a **rug** in front of the fire. Jill likes to sit on the **rug**. Pussy likes to sit on the **rug**, too.

Dad has a **rug** in the car. It is a car **rug**. Mother puts it over her knees to keep warm.

---

ruler

A **ruler** is a piece of wood or metal. It is sometimes marked off in inches or millimetres. We measure the length of things with a **ruler**. We draw straight lines with a **ruler**.

---

run

The cow and the pig have **run** away.
   The cow runs first.
      The pig runs after the cow.
         The dog is running after the pig.
            The farmer is running after the dog.

Who will **run** the fastest?

S S s

sack

The boys are running a **sack** race.

A **sack** is a big bag made of strong cloth. The farmer puts corn in a **sack**. The coal man puts coal in a **sack**.

sad

Pussy is lost. Jill is **sad**.
Pussy is found. Jill is glad.

saddle

This is Jack's **saddle**.
Jack puts his **saddle** on his pony's back.

safe

It is not **safe** to cross the street without looking. You will be in danger.

It is safer to look where you are going.

Safety first!

LOOK LEFT
SAFETY
FIRST

sail

Jack has gone for a **sail** on the **sea**.

The boat has a **sail** on it.

The wind blows on the **sail**, and sends the boat sailing along.

---

sailor

A **sailor** works on a ship. He sails on the sea.
Jack is going to be a **sailor**.
When he grows up, he will join the navy.

---

sale

Jack does not want to sell Spot.
Spot is not for **sale**. He is not to be sold.

---

salmon

A **salmon** is a large fish.
A **salmon** can leap out of the water.

---

salt

We use **salt** to make our food taste better.
Salt comes from **salt** mines under the ground.
There is **salt** in the sea. The sea is salty.

---

same

The cow has two calves. One calf is like the other calf. They are alike. They are the **same**.

The cow is not the **same** as the calves. She is different.

Santa Claus

Santa Claus brings lots of toys,
To lucky little girls and boys.

Santa Claus comes at Christmas time.
He is sometimes called Father Christmas or Saint Nicholas.

Saturday

Saturday is the last day in the week. We have a holiday from school every Saturday. There are seven days in a week. There are 7. Sunday, Monday, Tuesday, Wednesday, Thursday, Friday, Saturday.

saucer

We drink tea out of a cup.
We put the cup on a saucer.
We put the spoon in the saucer.

saw

Dad is going to saw some wood.
He wants to cut the wood into small bits.

He cuts the wood with a saw. He is sawing the wood.

When he has sawn the wood, there will be little bits left. They are like dust. They are called sawdust.

say

When you speak, you say words. You are saying words.
When you have spoken, you have said words.

scare

The crows got a **scare** when they saw a **scare**crow.
They got a fright. They were afraid of the **scare**crow.
The **scare**crow scares away the crows.

school

A **school** is a place where we learn to read and write.
We learn lessons in the **school**room.

scissors

Jill likes to cut out pictures. She cuts them with a pair of **scissors**. The **scissors** are sharp.

Scout

Here is a **Scout**. He wears a **Scout** uniform.

Here is a girl **Scout**. She is a Girl Guide. She wears a Guide uniform.

A **Scout** learns many useful things. He does a good deed every day.

sea

What fun we have at the **sea**!
We can paddle in the **sea**.
We can swim in the **sea**.
We can sail on the **sea**.

The **sea** is full of salty water. The water comes in to the shore in big waves. There are many fish in the **sea**.

seal

A **seal** lives in the sea. It can come out of the water and wriggle about on the land.

Jack and Jill saw a **seal** at the circus. It was doing tricks.

---

season

A **season** is one of the parts of the year. There are four parts in the year. There are four seasons. The seasons are spring, summer, autumn and winter.

---

seat

A **seat** is something to sit on.
A chair is a **seat**.
A bench in the park is a **seat**.

---

second

A **second** is a very short measure of time. There are sixty seconds in one minute. There are 60.

Sunday is the first day in the week. Monday is the **second**. **Second** is the one after first.

---

see

I **see** the Moon, and the Moon sees me,
God bless the Moon, and God bless me.

Jill looks with her eyes at the moon. She is seeing the moon. Jill has seen the moon before. She saw it last night.

Jack has gone to **see** Granny. He has gone to visit Granny.

seed

Most plants grow from a **seed**. We put seeds in the ground. We cover them over with earth. We are planting seeds. Soon the seeds begin to grow.

---

seesaw

Jack and Jill are on a **seesaw**. The **seesaw** moves up and down. When Jill is up, Jack is down. When Jack is up, Jill is down.

---

sell

What does the baker **sell**? The baker sells bread. You can buy bread from the baker.

---

send

Jack is in the Post Office. He is going to **send** a parcel to Granny. The postman will take the parcel away to Granny. Jack is sending it.

---

sense

When I was young and had no **sense**,
I bought a fiddle for eighteen pence.

Jack has **sense**. He does not do silly things. He is a sensible boy.

Jack has five senses. He has a **sense** of smell. He has a **sense** of touch. He has a **sense** of hearing. He has a **sense** of seeing. He has a **sense** of taste.

September

Warm **September** brings the fruit.
Sportsmen then begin to shoot.

September is the name of a month. There are twelve months in a year. There are 12.

January	February	March	April	May	June	July
1	2	3	4	5	6	7

August	September	October	November	December
8	9	10	11	12

---

seven

Seven is a number. It is **7**.
There are **seven** days in a week.
Here are **seven** bottles.

One	two	three	four	five	six	seven
1	2	3	4	5	6	7

---

sew

Mother can **sew** with a needle and thread.
She sews buttons on Jack's coat.
She sews dresses for Jill.
Jill is sewing a dress for her doll.

---

shade

It is a hot day. The cow is lying in the **shade**. She has found a cool place under a tree. The sun does not reach her. She is shaded from the sun.

she

Little Betty Pringle **she** had a pig.
It was not very little and not very big.

The pig was Betty's. It was **she** who owned the pig.
She was very fond of the pig. The pig would go everywhere **she** went.

---

sheep

A **sheep** is an animal. It has four legs. It has a woolly coat. Its coat is called a fleece.

A baby **sheep** is called a lamb. A man who looks after **sheep** is called a shepherd.

---

shelf

There are two shelves in the toy cupboard.
Jack's toys are on the top **shelf**.
Jill's toys are on the bottom **shelf**.

---

shell

A **shell** is the outside of anything. The outside of an egg is the **shell**. The outside of a nut is the **shell**.

---

ship

A **ship** is a big boat which sails on the water. There are many kinds of ships. There are battleships which are used in wars. There are liners, which are like floating hotels.

shoe

Jill has a left **shoe** and a right **shoe**.
She wears the left **shoe** on her left foot.
She wears the **right** shoe on her **right** foot.
She wears a pair of shoes.

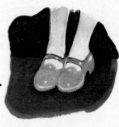

---

shop

Mother buys bread at the baker's **shop**.
Jill buys sweets at the sweet **shop**.
Jack buys a new ball at the toy **shop**
Dad buys new shoes in a shoe **shop**.

They all go shopping.

---

short

A minute is a **short** time.   A year is a long time.

Jill has a **short** stick.   Jack has a long stick.

---

shower

Hurry up !
Jack and Spot have been
caught in a **shower**.
A **shower** is light rain.

---

side

Jill is riding at the **side** of the road.   She is not in the middle of the road.

She has one leg on one **side** of her pony.   She has one leg on the other **side**.
Jill has a right **side** and a left **side**.

sight

Jack has good **sight**. He can see well.
It was a lovely **sight**. He saw a flock of wild geese.
Granny has bad **sight**.
She wears spectacles to help her to see better.

---

silly

The clown does **silly** things to make us laugh.
He falls over his feet. He stands on his head.
He is being **silly**.

---

silver

Silver is a metal. It looks white.
Some money is made of **silver**.
Mother has a **silver** teapot.
Jill has a **silver** ring.
Granny's hair is white. It looks like **silver**.

---

sing

I'll **sing** you a song,
Though not very long,
Yet I think it as pretty as any.
Put your hand in your purse,
You'll never be worse,
And give the poor singer a penny.

---

sink

Jack threw a stone in the pond.
He could see the stone **sink**.
The stone went down. It did not
float on the water. It had sunk.
Mother washes dishes at the **sink**.
The soap sinks into the water.

sit

The rabbits **sit** in a ring. One rabbit sits in the middle of the ring. The rabbits are all sitting. They have sat there for a long time.

six

Six is a number. Jill is **six** years old.
Six is half a dozen.

One	two	three	four	five	**six**
1	2	3	4	5	**6**

skate

Jack and Jill like to **skate** on the ice. They wear skates. The skates are on their boots. They slide over the ice. They are skating.

skin

Your body is covered with **skin**.
Animals and plants are covered with **skin,** too.
Peel off the **skin** before you eat the orange.

sleep

Baby is sleepy. He has gone to **sleep** in his cot. He is fast asleep. He has been sleeping for a long time. He has slept for hours.

slow

Granny cannot walk fast. She is **slow**. She walks slowly.
Jack is not **slow**. He is fast. He walks quickly.
The clock is **slow**. It has lost time.

---

small

Look at the three monkeys.
There is one very big monkey.
There is one not so big monkey.
It is smaller than the big
monkey. There is one very
small monkey. It is the
smallest of all.

---

smell

What are we having for dinner? Can you **smell** the food?
You can **smell** with your nose.

---

smile

There is a **smile** on Jill's face when she is happy.

Jill is crying.

Jill is smiling.

---

smoke

Smoke is like a little cloud. It comes from fire.
The **smoke** from the fire goes up the chimney.
Dad puffs **smoke** from his pipe when he is smoking.

snake

A **snake** has a long thin body. It has no legs. A **snake** can crawl along the ground. It can curl itself round and round. Some snakes can bite. There is poison in their bite.

snow

It is a snowy day. Jack and Jill are out in a **snow**storm. The **snow** is falling from the sky. It is frozen rain.

Jack and Jill are throwing **snow**balls. They are made of **snow**. They have made a **snow**man. He is made of **snow**. The **snow**flakes are falling. They are little pieces of **snow**.

soap

We use **soap** when we wash. It helps to make us clean. Jill has a bar of pink **soap**. Jack has a bar of white **soap**.

sock

A **sock** is a short stocking.
Jack wears one **sock** on his left foot.
He wears one **sock** on his right foot.
He wears a pair of socks.

soft

Pussy's fur is **soft** to touch.
A stone is not **soft**. It is hard.

soldier

A **soldier** is a man who fights for his country.
There are many soldiers in an army. Soldiers wear uniforms.
Jack has toy soldiers.

something

Granny has brought **something** for Jill. It is a present.
It is in her bag. It is **something** which she is going to give Jill.

son

A boy is the **son** of his father and mother.
Jack is the **son** of Dad and Mother.
Jill is their daughter.

song

Let us sing a **song**.
Let us sing words and music that match.

What **song** shall we sing?
Let us sing,
" Sing a **Song** of Sixpence."

soon

Jack and Jill are climbing a tree.
Jack will **soon** be at the top of the tree. He will be there in a short time. He will get there sooner than Jill. He will get there before Jill.

sound

What a lot of sounds we can hear with our ears!
We can hear the **sound** of Jack banging his drum.
We can hear the **sound** of Jill blowing her whistle.
We can hear the **sound** of the cow mooing.
Listen! What sounds can you hear?

south

There are four points of the earth.
They are north, **south**, east and
west.

Look at this map of Britain.
London is in the **south** of
Britain. It is the biggest
town in Britain.

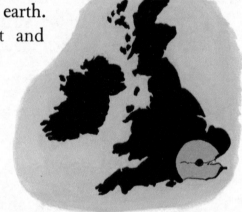

speak

Jill is speaking to the elephant.
She is saying words to him.
The elephant cannot **speak** to Jill.
He cannot say words, but he can
make a noise.

spell

Jack can **spell** his name. He can put the letters of his name
in the right order. He spells his name JACK BROWN.

spread

Spread the butter on the bread.
Cover the bread with butter.
Spread a cloth on the table.
Put the cloth all over the table.

spring

There are four parts of the year. There are four seasons.
The seasons are **spring**, summer, autumn and winter.

In **spring** the flowers begin
to grow. The birds build their
nests. The little lambs play
in the fields. They **spring**
about. They jump about on
their feet. **Spring**time is a
very happy time.

square

A thing that is **square** has four equal sides.
Jill's ball is round. Jill's brick is **square**.

squirrel

There was once a little **squirrel**.
He lived in a tree. He had a long,
bushy tail. He had sharp teeth.
He liked to eat nuts with his sharp
teeth. Before winter came, he
found a lot of nuts. He put the nuts in a heap. Then he fell
asleep. He slept all through the winter. The **squirrel** woke
up in spring. He was hungry. He began to eat his nuts.
He said, " What a clever **squirrel** I am ! "

stand

Jack can **stand** on his head.
Jill can **stand** on her feet.
Pussy is not standing.
She is sitting.

star

When the blazing sun is set,
And the grass with dew is wet,
Then you show your little light,
Twinkle, twinkle, all the night.

A **star** twinkles at night. You can see its light in the sky.
There are many stars in the sky.

station

Here is a railway **station**. This is where the trains stop.
Look at the people on the platform. They are waiting
for the train to come in. Some people will get out of the
train at the **station**. Some people will get into the train.
Then the train will go off to the next **station**.

stay

The train does not **stay** long at the station.
It will not be long at the station.
Jack is going away in the train to **stay** with Uncle Jack.
He is going to live with Uncle Jack.
He has stayed with Uncle Jack before.

---

steal

Pussy has jumped on the table.
She is going to **steal** some milk.
She is going to take something that
is not hers.

The bad man was put in prison
for stealing money.

---

steep

The hill is very **steep**. It is almost straight up.
It is a **steep** climb to get to the top.

---

step

Jack and Jill are walking.
They **step** out together.
Every time they put down their
feet, they take a **step**. Jill steps
lightly. Jack has stepped on a
stone.
They go up steps when they go
upstairs.

---

stick

A **stick** is a thin piece of wood. We use sticks to light the
fire. We **stick** a stamp on a letter. We put the stamp on
the letter. The stamp has stuck to the letter.

still

Let me see if Philip can
Be a little gentleman.
Let me see if he is able
To sit **still** for once at table.

When we sit **still**, we sit without moving.
Philip is **still** sitting **still**. He has not moved up to now.

---

sting

A wasp can **sting**.
It can hurt you with its **sting**.
Jill was once stung by a wasp.
She felt a stinging pain.

---

stomach

Your **stomach** is part of your body. It is where your food
goes when you swallow it.

---

stop

Stop ! Dad sees the red light.
He must **stop** his car. He must
not go on.
He has stopped his car. He
will **stop** there till the light
changes. He will stay there.
He is stopping.

---

story

Jill is reading a **story** in her **story** book.
The **story** is called " Snow White."
" Black Beauty " is the **story** of a horse.
" Bambi " is the **story** of a deer.
Do you know any stories ?

straight

The ducks are swimming in a **straight** line.

The birds are not flying in a **straight** line. They are not in an even line.

street

A **street** is a road in a town.
There are shops in the street.
The **street** is very busy. Buses and cars go along the **street**.
Sometimes there are accidents in the **street**.
Take care how you cross the **street**.

string

String is thin cord. We tie things with **string**.

strong

This man is very **strong**. He is not weak. He can carry a heavy load.
He has great strength.
On stormy days, a **strong** wind blows.
A **strong** wind is called a gale.
We use **strong** string to tie up parcels.

such

Spot is **such** a clever dog.
He is a very clever dog.
He does **such** clever tricks.
Jack took **such** pains to teach him.

S s s

sugar

Sugar is sweet. We put **sugar** in food to make it sweet. **Sugar** comes from a plant called the **sugar** cane. It is also made from **sugar** beets.

---

summer

Summer is one of the parts of the year. There are four parts in the year. There are four seasons. The seasons are spring, **summer**, autumn and winter.

---

sun

Look at the **sun**. It is shining in the sky. It gives us light. It gives us heat. It gives us sunshine. It is a sunny day. The **sun** shines through the day. The moon shines at night.

Sunday

As Tommy Snooks and Bessy Brooks
Were walking out on **Sunday**,
Says Tommy Snooks to Bessy Brooks,
" Tomorrow will be Monday."

Sunday is the first day in the week.
There are seven days in a week. There are 7.

Sunday	Monday	Tuesday	Wednesday
1	2	3	4

Thursday	Friday	Saturday.
5	6	7

---

suppose

I **suppose** we will have honey for tea.
I think perhaps we might have honey.

sure   I am **sure** we have had honey for tea. I know we have had honey. I ate some honey, so I am quite **sure**.

---

surprise   Jack is hiding behind the tree.
Jill does not know he is there.
He is going to **surprise** Jill.
Jill will be surprised to see him.

---

swallow   We put food in our mouth. We chew it. Then we **swallow** the food. When we have swallowed the food, it goes into our stomach.
There is a bird called a **swallow**. The **swallow** goes to warm countries in the winter. Early in the year the **swallow** comes back to Britain.

---

sweet   Things made with sugar are **sweet**. Sweets are **sweet**. Honey is **sweet**. Jam is **sweet**. A rose has a **sweet** smell.

---

swim      Jack can travel through the water.
He can **swim**.
He is swimming.
Fish **swim**. Ducks and swans **swim**. Can you **swim**?

Jack has been able to **swim** since he was a little boy.

T t *t*

table

A **table** is very useful.
We put things on the **table**.
We sit at the **table** at meal times.
A **table** is flat on top. It has four legs.
Jill's dolls are having tea at the **table**.
The teapot is on the **table**.

tail

Jill is trying to catch hold of Pussy's **tail**.
Most animals and birds have tails.
This monkey uses its **tail** when climbing trees.

take

Dad is going to **take** Jack and Jill to the sea.
He will make them come with him to the sea.
Jill will **take** Dad's hand. She will hold his hand.
They will **take** a bus. They will ride on the bus.
It will **take** an hour to go. It will need an hour to go.
Jack will **take** his spade with him. He will carry his spade.
Jill will **take** off her hat. She will lift it off.

talk

Jill talks to the baby.
She says words to the baby.
She has talked to the baby.
The baby cannot **talk** yet.
She cannot say words.
When she is older she will
learn to **talk**.
She will soon be talking.

tall

A giant is very **tall**. A dwarf is very short.
Jack is taller than Jill. Dad is taller than Jack.
Dad is the tallest.

tame

Pussy is a **tame** animal. She is
not wild.   The tiger is a wild
animal. It is not **tame**. Pussy is
glad that the tiger is in a cage.
She knows the tiger is not **tame**.

tea

Molly, my sister, and I fell out,
And what do you think it was all about?
She loved coffee and I loved **tea**,
And that was the reason we couldn't agree.

We drink **tea**. We pour boiling water on **tea** leaves.
The **tea** leaves come from the **tea** plant.

teach

Jack and Jill go to school to learn things.
The teachers are there to **teach** them.
The teachers show them how to read and write.
Jack likes to **teach** Spot tricks. He shows Spot how to do tricks. He is teaching Spot.
Spot likes to be taught to do tricks.

---

team

A **team** is two or more people or animals, who are doing the same things.
Here is a **team** of horses.
Jack plays in a cricket **team**.
He plays with a **team** of boys.
Jill plays in a hockey **team**.
She plays with a **team** of girls.

---

tear

Jill has torn her frock. There is a **tear** in it. The **tear** is a hole. Mother will mend the **tear**.
She tore her frock yesterday. She made a hole in her frock yesterday.
She will get a new frock in a parcel. She will **tear** the paper off the parcel. She will pull the paper off the parcel.
She must be careful not to **tear** her new frock.

---

tear

This word is spelt the same as the one before. But it has not the same meaning. This **tear** is water which comes from your eyes. When you cry, there are tears in your eyes. You are in tears.

tease

Spot is trying to **tease** Pussy.
He is trying to annoy her.

Speak roughly to your little boy,
And beat him when he sneezes.
He only does it to annoy,
Because he knows it teases.

telephone

Mother is speaking to Dad on the **telephone**. Can you see Dad? No, Dad is far away in London. Mother cannot see him, but she can hear his voice. The **telephone** takes her voice over the **telephone** wire. Dad can hear her voice.

tell

I'll **tell** you a tale
About a whale,
Who told a lie
And went to jail.

Tell me a story about a whale.
Say to me what the whale did.
The whale told a lie. He said a thing that was not true.
He was telling lies. So he was sent to jail.

ten

Ten is a number.
Jill has **ten** fingers. Jill has **ten** toes. She has **10**.
Five and five make **ten**.

One two three four five six seven eight nine **ten**
1   2   3   4   5   6   7   8   9   **10**

tent

Jack is a Cub. He goes to camp. When he is in camp, he lives in a **tent**. The **tent** is made of canvas. It is held in place by **tent** pegs. It is great fun to sleep in a **tent**.

than

Dad's car can go faster **than** Jack's bicycle.
Jack would rather have a bicycle **than** a car. Dad's car is passing Jack's bicycle.

thank

Mother has given Jill a skipping-rope.
" **Thank** you, Mother," says Jill. Jill is thanking Mother. She is glad to have it. She is thankful to Mother.

that

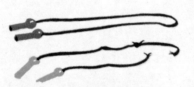

This is Jill's new skipping-rope. **That** is her old one. You can see **that** her old one is broken.

This is the dog
That bit the thief
For stealing all
His master's beef.

This is the cat
That killed the cock
For waking her
At five o'clock.

these

These toys are Jack's.   **These** toys are Jill's.

---

they

Once upon a time there were Three Bears.
They lived in a little house in the wood.
They each had a chair.
They each had a bed.
They each had a bowl of porridge.

---

thick

The Three Bears lived in a **thick** wood. The trees grew close together in the wood. The walls in their house were **thick**. They were not thin. The Three Bears liked **thick** porridge.

---

thief

The Knave of Hearts was a **thief**.
He stole the tarts away.
Thieves are put in prison.
People who steal things are put in prison.

---

thimble

Mother puts a **thimble** on the end of her finger when she sews. She puts the **thimble** on her middle finger. She pushes the needle into her **sewing** with her **thimble**.

thin

Tommy would not eat his dinner.
Every day he's growing thinner.

Tommy is **thin**. He is not fat.
A needle is **thin**. A wall is thick.

This is a **thin** boy.   This is a fat boy.

---

think

Think before you speak. You **think** with your mind.
Jill reads stories. Then she thinks about them.
Jill thinks that Jack is a nice boy.
She believes he is a nice boy.
Jack thought it was going to snow.
He believed it was going to snow.

---

third

Three little pigs ran a race.
There was a pink pig. The pink pig was first.
There was a spotted pig. The spotted pig was second.
There was a black pig. The black pig was **third**.

those

Those birds at the top of the tree are crows.
These birds under the tree are hens.
Those birds up there are black.
These birds down below are white.

three

Look at the **three** bears.
There are two real bears.
There is one teddy bear.
Two and one make **three**.
The third bear is the teddy bear.

throat

The **throat** is the front part of the neck.
It is also the place where you swallow.
Jack wears a scarf round his **throat** on cold days.
If he forgets his scarf, he might get a sore **throat**.

through

Mother pulls the thread **through** the eye of a needle.
She puts it in at one side, and pulls it out of the other side.
She has pulled the thread **through**.

The moon shines **through** the night.
It shines during the night.
The moon shines **through** the window.
It shines in at the window.

throw

Look at the cowboy. His horse is going to **throw** him off. The horse is going to make him fall off. He will be thrown off.

Jack can **throw** a ball. One day he threw a ball over the house.

---

thumb

You have two thumbs. You have one **thumb** on your left hand. You have one **thumb** on your right hand. The **thumb** is the thickest of your fingers.

Thursday

Thursday is one of the days in the week. There are seven days in a week. There are 7.

Sunday	Monday	Tuesday	Wednesday
1	2	3	4
	Thursday	Friday	Saturday.
	5	6	7

---

ticket

A **ticket** is a little card.
We buy a bus **ticket** when we ride on the bus.
We buy a train **ticket** when we ride on the train.

---

tie

Can you **tie** a knot ?
The farmer has tied the bull to the fence.
Dad wears a **tie** round his neck.
Jack ties up a parcel with string.
He is good at tying knots.

tiger

A **tiger** is a wild animal. It is like a very big cat.
You can see a **tiger** in the zoo.

There once was a lady of Riga,
Who went for a ride on a **tiger**.
They returned from the ride
With the lady inside
And a smile on the face of the **tiger**.

time

What **time** is it?
It is **time** to get up.
Jill wants to be in **time** for school.
She can tell the **time** by looking at
the clock.

tiny

A fly is very small. It is **tiny**.
Tom Thumb was very **tiny**.
Can you think of something else that is **tiny**?

tired

Dad has worked hard all day. He is **tired**.
He sits in his chair to have a rest. Then he is not **tired**
any longer. He is ready to play with Jack and Jill.

to

To market, **to** market, a gallop, a trot,
To buy some meat **to** put in the pot.

The old man is going **to** market.
He is going because he wants meat.
He is going **to** market **to** buy meat.

today Today is this day. Yesterday is the day before today. Tomorrow is the day after today.

toe 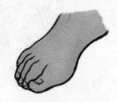 You have five toes on each foot. You have 5. You have one big toe on each foot. You have four smaller toes on each foot.

together Jack and Jill have gone for a walk together. Jack is with Jill. Jill is with Jack. They are together.

tomato Do you know what colour a tomato is? It is green when it is not ripe. It is red when it is ripe. A tomato is a vegetable.

tomorrow Tomorrow is the day after today. If this is Sunday, tomorrow will be Monday.

tongue Where is your tongue? Your tongue is in your mouth. What use is your tongue? You taste with your tongue. You speak with your tongue.

tonight Jill goes to school today. Tonight she is going to bed. Tonight is the night of today.

too

Can you see a fairy?
Can you see an elf, **too**?
Can you see an elf also?
The elf's shoes are **too** big for him.
They are more than big enough.

---

tooth

Jill goes to the dentist when she has **tooth**ache.
She goes to the dentist when one of her teeth aches.
Jill's teeth are white. Jill chews with her teeth.

---

top

Look at the cock on **top** of the steeple. It is very high up. It is as high as the **top** of the hill.
Jack has a toy called a **top**.
He can spin the **top** round and round.

---

town

Wee Willie Winkie
Runs through the **town**,
Upstairs and downstairs
In his nightgown.

A **town** is a small city. There are streets and shops in a **town**.
Jack and Jill live in a **town**.
Uncle Jack lives in the country.

---

toy

A **toy** is a thing to play with. Jack has a kite. He has tin soldiers. He has a bow and arrow. They are his toys.

train

Jack and Jill are on the bridge. They are watching the **train**. The **train** is on the railway line. Some trains carry people. Some trains carry goods.

tree

A **tree** is a very big plant. There are many trees in a wood. There are oak trees, and ash trees and elm trees.

trip

Look at Jack. He is going to **trip** over Pussy. He is going to catch his foot against Pussy. He will tumble over her. He has tripped over Pussy before.

Dad and Mother have gone for a **trip** to the sea. They have gone on a short journey to the sea.

true

A lie is something that is not **true**. It is not **true** to say that Jack is a girl. It is **true** to say that Jack is a boy. Always say what is **true**. Always tell the truth.

trunk

This is the **trunk** of an elephant. It is the elephant's long nose.

This is the **trunk** we pack our clothes in when we go on holiday.

The stem of a tree is called a tree **trunk**.

try

Jill is going to **try** to catch Neddy, the donkey. She is not sure that she can catch Neddy. She is going to **try**.

Tuesday

Tuesday is one of the days of the week. There are seven days in a week. There are 7.

Sunday   Monday   **Tuesday**   Wednesday
Thursday   Friday   Saturday.

---

tug

A **tug** is a little ship. It helps to pull a big ship into dock. It tugs the big ship.
Jack plays **tug**-of-war. He tugs the rope. He gives it a strong pull. He is tugging it.

---

tulip

A **tulip** is a spring flower. It grows from a bulb. You can grow tulips in many different colours.

---

tumble

Jack fell down and broke his crown,
And Jill came tumbling after.

A **tumble** is a fall. Teddy Bear tumbled downstairs.

---

tune

The only **tune** that he could play Was over the hills and far away.

A **tune** is like a little story in music. Jill can play tunes on the piano. Can you sing a **tune**?

turkey

A **turkey** is a big bird. Uncle Jack has turkeys on the farm.
They say, " Gobble, gobble, gobble."
We eat **turkey** on Christmas Day.

turn

Jill is having a ride on Neddy.
It will be Jack's **turn** next.
Neddy will **turn** round when he comes to the fence.
The sun has come out. It has turned very warm.

Mother turns on the tap to get water.
Jill likes turning over the pages of her story book.

turnip

A **turnip** is a vegetable.
Dad grows turnips in the garden.
Mother cooks turnips for dinner.
Uncle Jack grows turnips on his farm.
Cows and sheep like to eat turnips.

twelve

Twelve is a number. It is **12**.
Can you count up to **twelve**?
A dozen is **twelve**.
There are **twelve** eggs in a dozen eggs.
Two sixes make **twelve**.
There are a dozen eggs in the basket.

twenty   Twenty is a number. It is **20**. Two tens make **twenty**.

---

twin   Here are two little boys who look alike. They are brothers. They were born on the same day. They are the same age. They are twins.

Peter	David
Peter is David's **twin**.	David is Peter's **twin**.

---

two   Two little dogs
Sat by the fire,
Over a fender of coal dust.
Said one little dog
To the other little dog,
" If you don't talk, why, I must."

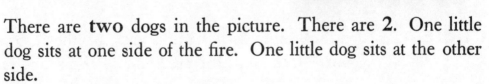

There are **two** dogs in the picture. There are **2**. One little dog sits at one side of the fire. One little dog sits at the other side.
One and one make **two**.
Jill has **two** hands. She has **two** feet.

---

tyre   Dad's car has four wheels.
It has a rubber **tyre** on each wheel.
It has four tyres.

U u *u*

ugly

Cinderella had two **ugly** sisters. They were not pretty. Cinderella was pretty. She was not **ugly**. The **Ugly** Sisters were unkind to Cinderella.

umbrella

It is a wet day. Mother has gone to shop. She has taken her **umbrella** with her. She puts up the **umbrella**. The **umbrella** shelters her from the rain. Dad has a big **umbrella**. Jill has a little **umbrella**.

uncle

Dad's brother is **Uncle** Jack. Mother's brother is **Uncle** Tom. Jack and Jill are fond of their uncles.

under

The dog jumps over the fence. The pig crawls **under** the fence. The dog is above. The pig is below. The pig is **under** the dog.

understand

Spot seems to **understand** every word Jack says. He seems to know what Jack says.
Dad understands how the radio works. He found out how it worked. Then he understood it.

---

unhappy

When Jill is happy, she laughs and sings.
When she is **unhappy**, she looks sad and cries.
Jill was **unhappy** when she lost Pussy.
She was happy when she found Pussy.

---

uniform

Jack wears a Cub **uniform**. He is dressed the same as the other Cubs. They all wear **uniforms**. Jill wears a Brownie **uniform**.

Soldiers wear **uniform**.   Airmen wear **uniform**.

Sailors wear **uniform**.   Postmen wear **uniform**.

---

unkind

The Ugly Sisters were **unkind** to Cinderella. They were not kind to her. They said **unkind** things to her. They treated her unkindly.

unless Jack must not go out **unless** he has his shoes on.
He must not go out if he has not his shoes on.

---

unselfish

Jill has a box of chocolates.
She is not going to keep them to herself. That would be selfish.
She is sharing them with Jack and Pat.
Jill is an **unselfish** girl.
She is not selfish.

---

until Jack will not go to bed **until** eight o'clock.
He will not go to bed up to the time of eight o'clock.

---

unusual It is **unusual** to see a cow riding a bicycle. It is not usual. It is an **unusual** sight. A cow does not usually ride a bicycle.

---

up Jack gets **up** in the morning. He gets out of bed.
He stands **up**. He stands on his feet.
He climbs **up** a tree. He climbs to the highest part of the tree.

When they were **up**, they were **up**,
And when they were down, they were down,
But when they were only half-way **up**,
They were neither **up** nor down.

upon

Upon means up on.

Pussy sits **upon** a chair.
Pussy sits up on a chair.

Upon Paul's steeple stands a tree,
As full of apples as may be.
The little boys of London town,
They run with hooks and pull them down.

---

upstairs

Upstairs, downstairs,
And in my lady's chamber.

Jill goes **upstairs** when she goes up the stairs.
She comes downstairs when she comes down the stairs.

---

us

Jill is alone. She says, " Look at me. I am alone."
Jill is with Jack. She says, " Look at **us**. Look at me, and somebody else."

---

use

We **use** our hands for lifting things. We **use** our feet for walking. We **use** a pencil for writing. These are useful things. We can do things with them.
Jack is used to Spot. Spot is used to Jack. They know each other. They are not strangers.
What is the **use** of being cross ? There is no need to be cross. It does not do any good.

V V *v*

valley   Can you see the river down in the **valley**? A **valley** is a place between hills. It is the low ground between hills.

van   A **van** is a car that is made to carry a load.
A mail **van** carries letters and parcels.
A furniture **van** carries furniture.
A luggage **van** is a coach on a train.
We put our trunks in the luggage **van**.

vase   Mother is putting flowers in a **vase**. She puts water in the **vase** first. The water keeps the flowers alive.

vegetable   A **vegetable** is a plant that we can eat. Potatoes are vegetables. Turnips and beans are vegetables. Dad grows vegetables in the garden. Mother cooks them for dinner.

velvet   **Velvet** is a soft cloth. It is smooth to touch.
Jill has a dress made of **velvet**.
When you touch a pansy, it feels like **velvet**.

---

verse   A **verse** is a short piece of poetry. Here is a **verse**.

" Will you walk a little faster ? "
Said a whiting to a snail.
" There's a porpoise close behind us,
And he's treading on my tail."

very   Jill is **very** fond of ice-cream. She likes it **very** much.
It is **very** cold and **very** sweet.

---

view   Jack and Jill are at the top of
a hill. They are looking at
the **view**. They can see a
village down below. They
can see hills in the distance.
It is a lovely **view**.

---

village   A **village** is a small town. A city is a big town.
London is not a **village**. It is a city.

---

vine   A **vine** is a plant. It can trail along the ground.
It can climb. Grapes grow on the grape **vine**.
They grow in bunches on the grape **vine**.

violet

A **violet** is a flower. There are wild violets, which grow in the woods. There are violets which grow in the garden. **Violet** is a colour. It is like the colour of the flower of the same name. **Violet** is pale purple.

violin

We can make music on the **violin**.
A **violin** is sometimes called a fiddle. Jack is learning to play the **violin**. He can play some tunes on it.
A man who plays the **violin** is called a violinist.

visit

Jill has gone to see Granny. She has gone to **visit** Granny. Jill likes visiting Granny. Granny gives her honey for tea.

visitor

Someone has come to visit Granny.
Granny has a **visitor**.
Who is the **visitor**? Is it Jill?
Jill has come to tea.

voice

'Tis the **voice** of the lobster,
I heard him declare,
"You have baked me too brown,
I must sugar my hair."

You make words with your mouth. You talk with your **voice**. You sing and shout with your **voice**.

W W _W_

wade

Jill likes to **wade** at the sea-side. She walks in the water. She skips about, over the waves. Spot likes wading, too. Jack is not wading. He is having a swim.

wagon

A **wagon** can carry heavy loads. It has four wheels. Uncle Jack has a **wagon** on his farm. He carries hay in his **wagon**.
A railway truck is called a **wagon**.

wait

Jack and Jill **wait** for the aeroplane to land. They stay where they are till the aeroplane lands.
Mother is waiting for them at home. She will **wait** till they come. She will stay there until they come home.

wall

Pussy sits on the garden **wall**.

Roses grow up the **wall** of the house.

Jill has pictures on her bedroom **wall**.

---

warm

It is a **warm** day. The sun is shining. We do not feel cold. It is **warm** in the sun. It is **warm** by the fire.

---

was

The maid **was** in the garden Hanging out the clothes.

The maid is not in the garden now. She **was** there long ago.

Jill **was** at school this morning. She **was** a good girl all day. She has been a good girl all day.

---

wash

The maid washed the clothes. Then she hung them out to dry. It was washing-day.
Jill can **wash** her doll's clothes.
She can **wash** herself with soap and water.
She makes herself clean, when she washes herself.

---

wasp

A **wasp** is an insect. It has four wings. It can sting. It has black and yellow stripes on its body.

waste

I must not throw upon the floor
The crust I cannot eat.
For many little hungry ones
Would think it quite a treat.

We must not **waste** food. It is a **waste** to throw it away. Jack does not **waste** his money. He does not spend his money on foolish things. **Waste** not, want not.

---

watch

Grandpa has an old-fashioned pocket **watch**. Mother wears a **watch** on her wrist. You can tell the time by looking at a **watch**.
Watch how the hands go round on the **watch**. Look at the **watch** and you will see the hands move.
Jill watches for Dad coming home at night. She looks out of the window to see if he is coming.

---

water

The pond is full of **water**. The sea is full of **water**. Jack gets wet when he swims in the **water**. He drinks **water** when he is thirsty.

---

way

The little girl is crying. She has lost her **way**. She cannot find her **way** home.
The policeman will help her. He knows the **way**. He will take her home. It is not a long **way**. It is not far.

we

The little girl was lost. She was all by herself. She cried, " I am lost." Then the policeman came. She was not alone. Somebody was with her. He said, " **We** will soon find the way home. You and I will find it."

---

wear

Jill is going to a party. She will **wear** a new dress. She will put on a new dress.
She is wearing an old dress now.
She has worn it often.
She wore it yesterday.

---

weed

Dad is weeding the garden.
He is taking out the weeds.
A **weed** is a wild plant.
Dad does not want weeds to grow in the garden. They choke the other plants, so that they cannot grow.

---

week

There are seven days in a **week**.
There are four weeks in a month.
There are fifty-two weeks in a year. There are 52.
Do you know the names of the seven days in the **week** ?

Of all the days that's in the **week**
I dearly love but one day—
And that's the day that comes betwixt
A Saturday and Monday.

Can you tell what day of the **week** that is ?

weigh

Jill is going to **weigh** herself. She is going to see how heavy she is. She is going to find out her weight. Do you know how to **weigh** yourself?

well

Ding, dong, bell,
Pussy's in the **well**.
Who put her in?
Little Tommy Thin.
Who pulled her out?
Little Tommy Stout.

The **well** is full of water. It is a deep hole with water in it. Pussy does not feel **well**. She has been in the water. She feels ill. She will sit by the fire, and will soon get **well**. She will be **well** looked after. She will be treated kindly. Pussy can do tricks **well**. She is good at doing tricks.

west

There are four points of the earth.
They are north, south, east and **west**.
The sun sets in the **west**.

The south wind brings wet weather,
The north wind wet and cold together.
The **west** wind always brings us rain,
The east wind blows it back again.

wet

It is raining. It is a **wet** day.
Jack gets **wet** when he goes swimming.

whale A **whale** is the biggest creature in the sea.

A **whale** has to come up to the surface to breathe. Some whales spout water up into the air when they breathe.

---

wheel Jill is wheeling the pram.
She is pushing the pram.
The pram goes on wheels.
Each **wheel** is round.
Dad's car has four wheels.
Jack's bicycle has two wheels.
There is one **wheel** on the **wheelbarrow**.

---

where **Where** does the Queen live?
In what place does the Queen live?
Kings and queens live in palaces.
That is **where** they live.

---

whether

Jack is buying a new toy car. He does not know **whether** to buy the blue one or **whether** to buy the red one. He does not know which one to choose.

whistle

Can you **whistle** a tune?
Can you make music with your lips?
Can you hear the birds whistling?
The guard blows his **whistle**.

who

Who is Jack's sister? Jill is the girl **who** is Jack's sister.

whose

Whose turn is it to go into the middle of the ring?
It is the little Dutch boy's turn.

Whose hat is Spot wearing?
He is wearing the little Dutch boy's hat.

why

Why is the little Dutch boy in the middle of the ring?
The reason is that it is his turn to be in the middle.

wide

The door of the cow shed is **wide** open. It is a **wide** door. It is not narrow. It is **wide** enough for the cows to go in.
A pin is narrow. It is not **wide**.
The sea is **wide**.

win

Who will **win** the race? Who will get there first?

Will the duck **win**? Will the lamb **win**?
Will the pig **win**? Will Pussy **win**?

---

wing

A bird has two wings. It flies with its wings. Each **wing** has feathers on it.
An insect has wings. A butterfly has wings.
An aeroplane has wings.

---

winter

Winter is one of the seasons of the year. There are four seasons. They are spring, summer, autumn and **winter**.
Winter is the coldest season. Snow comes in **winter**.

---

wish

I **wish** I lived in a caravan,
With a horse to drive, like a pedlar-man!

I **wish** you a Merry Christmas.
I hope you will have a Merry Christmas.
Jack wishes a **wish**. He wishes it were Christmas Day.

with

The man in the caravan is **with** the horse.
He and the horse are together.

---

without

Jill has gone out with her
shoes on.
Jack has gone out **without**
his shoes.
He has no shoes on his feet.

---

woman

Mother is a **woman**. Jill is a little girl. When Jill grows
up she will be a **woman**. Mother and Jill will be women.

---

wood

The Three Bears lived in a little house in the **wood**. There
are many trees in a **wood**. We get **wood** from trees. The
table is made of **wood**. It is wooden.

---

work

What a busy family! Everybody is working.
Dad's **work** is digging in the garden.
Mother's **work** is hanging out the clothes.

Jack's **work** is washing Spot. Jill's **work** is feeding hens.

world　The **world** is the place we live in. It is the whole earth and the sky.

---

worth

Dad has bought Jack a toy train. It is **worth** fifty pence. It cost fifty pence.

Jill has a new book. It is full of good stories. It is well **worth** reading.

Mother has bought five pence **worth** of ice-cream. She has paid five pence for ice-cream.

---

write　Jill can **write**. She can put words on paper. We can read the words she writes. She can **write** a letter to Uncle Jack. She begins by writing, " Dear Uncle Jack."

---

wrong　What is **wrong** with this picture?
What is not right in the picture?

It is **wrong** to tell a lie. It is right to tell the truth.

X x *x*

X

X is a letter. We do not use it often at the beginning of a word. We use **X** in words like o**x**, bo**x**, fo**x**, a**x**e, and e**x**tra.

Xmas

Sometimes we spell Christmas like **Xmas**. This is what happens at **Xmas**.

Jack and Jill hang up their stockings on **Xmas** Eve.

Santa Claus comes down the chimney and puts toys in the stockings.

Jack and Jill play with the toys.

They have a party and a **Xmas** Tree.

Y y *y*

yard   A **yard** is a measure of length. A **yard** is a little shorter than a metre. A **yard** is also a small piece of ground. There is a fence or wall round the **yard.**

yellow   Yellow is a colour. This is **yellow.**

A banana is **yellow.**

A buttercup is **yellow.**

The monkey is wearing a **yellow** jacket.

you   Jack asks, " Are **you** coming out to play, Jill ? "
Mother says, " **You** children must not go out. **You** must do your sums, Jill. **You** must feed Spot, Jack."

young   If you are **young**, you are not old.
A **young** child is called a baby.
A **young** cow is called a calf.
A **young** cat is called a kitten.
A **young** dog is called a puppy.
A **young** hen is called a chicken.